Traveling Light

Reflections on the Free Life

Eugene H. Peterson

InterVarsity Press
Downers Grove
Illinois 60515

InterVarsity Press is the book-publishing division of Inter-Varsity Christian Fellowship, a student movement active on campus at hundreds of universities, colleges and schools of nursing. For information about local and regional activities, write IVCF, 233 Langdon St., Madison, WI 53703.

Distributed in Canada through InterVarsity Press, 1875 Leslie St., Unit 10, Don Mills, Ontario M3B 2M5, Canada.

Cover photograph: Gary Irving

ISBN 0-87784-377-5

Printed in the United States of America

Library of Congress Cataloging in Publication Data

Peterson, Eugene H., 1932-
   Traveling light.

   Bibliography: p.
   1. Freedom (Theology) 2. Bible. N.T. Galatians
—Criticism, interpretation, etc. I. Title.
BT810.2.P4   233'.7   82-15314
ISBN 0-87784-377-5   AACR2

17	16	15	14	13	12	11	10	9	8	7	6	5	4	3	2	1
96	95	94	93	92	91	90	89	88	87	86	85	84	83	82		

For Valerie

If you hold to my teaching, you are really my disciples. Then you will know the truth, and the truth will set you free. . . . So if the Son sets you free, you will be free indeed.

John 8:31-32, 36 NIV

We join our prayers today in intercession for men and women in our society who are trapped:

> *those who are trapped in poverty with no sign of relief;*
> *those who are trapped in jobs that engage but a fraction of their powers;*
> *those who are trapped in families where love has ebbed away;*
> *those who are trapped in unwanted alliances out of which they cannot break;*
> *those who are trapped by the fear of discovery, or by dependency on others; or by the need for drugs, or by an addiction to alcohol.*

O Thou whose will it is that we be free, and who didst give Thy Son that we might be delivered from all coercive powers;
make us examples of Thy freedom, proclaimers of Thy freedom, and instruments of Thy freedom;
snap our chains that we may loose the chains of others.

Then shall the joy of the liberated rise from the earth like a mighty hymn of praise, Through Jesus Christ our Lord. Amen.

Ernest T. Campbell[1]

---

1 Free for All

W E LIVE IN A WORLD awash in fantasies of freedom. We spend enormous sums of money and immense amounts of psychic energy on these fantasies. We fantasize a free life based variously on power, on sex, on fame, on leisure. Whole industries develop out of these fantasies. Careers are shaped by them. Political movements are launched and fueled by them. But the world we live in is conspicuously and sadly lacking in the *experience* of freedom. The fantasies are barren: they give birth to nothing in word or deed. For all our elaborate and expensive fantasies, the actual lives that most people live are filled with impotence, boredom, obscurity, and hassle.

Living in the land of the free has not made us free; we are a nation of addicts and complainers. Being provided with freedom of religion has not made us free; coercive cults and enslaving superstitions continue to proliferate.

Assembling with people in church and listening to ringing proclamations of freedom—"He whom the Son sets free is free indeed!"—has not made us free. Our churches are attended regularly by the inhibited, the obsessive-compulsive, the fearfully defensive—enough of them to provide outside observers with a stereotype.

But not everything that has to do with freedom is fantasy. There are also realities of freedom. They are not, perhaps, as conspicuous, but they are there, at least for people of faith. These people believe that God is free. He created the world and the people in it freely and not out of necessity. Since a free God is at the center of all existence, and all creation and every creature issues from a free act, freedom and not necessity is always the deeper and more lasting reality. At the center of that belief is the story of Jesus, the freest person who ever lived. And there is recurrent witness of the Spirit who is free, like the wind that "blows where it wills." In every culture and land there is abundant testimony that persons who trust in God participate in this freedom. My own experience supports the testimony: when I live in faith I live freely. When I set God at the center of my life, I realize vast freedoms and surprising spontaneities. When I center life in my own will, my freedom diminishes markedly. I live constricted and anxious.

I live in a vortex where these fantasies and realities mingle. The life I live in the world cannot escape the fantasies, but neither can it avoid the realities. Like so many others who have chosen to live by faith, I find that it is a daily task to discriminate between the fantasies and the realities. And I need all the help I can get.

Truth in Need of Focus

There are moments when a single truth seems to cry out for focused proclamation. For me one of these moments came in the early 1980s; freedom in Christ seemed the truth in need of focus. The end of a millennium was in sight. It would soon be two thousand years since Christ lived and died and rose again. The world had seen a succession of political and social revolutions that had featured the word *freedom*. Especially in the Western world, but hardly confined there, aspirations to freedom were very strong. But when I looked at the people I was living with as pastor—fairly affluent, well educated, somewhat knowledgeable about the Christian faith—I realized how unfree they were. They were buying expensive security systems to protect their possessions from burglary. They were overcome with anxieties in the face of rising inflation. They were pessimistic about the prospects for justice and peace in a world bristling with sophisticated weapons systems and nuclear devices. They were living huddled, worried, defensive lives. I wanted to shout in objection: Don't live that way! You are Christians! Our lives can be a growth into freedom instead of a withdrawal into anxious wariness.

Instead of shouting I returned to my regular round of work—preaching and teaching, visiting and counseling, praying and writing, encouraging and directing—but I was determined to seek ways in which I could awaken a hunger and thirst for the free life among people who had lost an appetite for it, and then, having awakened the appetite, to find the food and drink that would satisfy it. The more I did this, the more I became convinced that the experience of freedom in the life of faith is at the very heart of what it means to be human.

No truth is ever out of date, and none should be promoted at the expense of the whole truth, but there are occasions when particular truths must be emphasized. Is this such a time? Just as the fourth century required an emphasis on the deity of Christ, and the sixteenth century an emphasis on justification by faith, perhaps these last years of the twentieth century need an emphasis on the freedom that comes to maturity in a life of faith in Christ. Maybe living out this Christ-freedom is a gift we can offer the world as it approaches its millennial milestone. So that is what I set myself to do.

Slogans and Cant
In the process of doing this work I encountered difficulties. For instance, there was the matter of terminology. The word *freedom,* once a vessel light and swift, has become barnacle-encrusted with slogans and cant, sluggish in the waters of discourse, unresponsive to nuance or insight. For centuries philosophers and theologians and poets kept the world clean in the service of truth. But in recent decades it has been appropriated by people who want to sell ideas and things for a profit, quite apart from any interest in truth.

Political propagandists and advertising copy writers have a monopoly on the word. If someone wants to use it to say something carefully and truly about persons or God, who has ears to hear? The word is immensely attractive and awakens such deep longings in us that it is no wonder that those who want us to buy their goods or enlist in their projects make promises of freedom.

The word *freedom* is used with deliberate cynicism by many to disguise operations that are enslaving. It is also used carelessly and thoughtlessly by others so that it has long since lost connection with truths that root experience in reality. Shouting the word *freedom* does nothing to bring about its reality. Labeling thoughts or actions as free does not alter their actual nature. Freedom is not an abstraction, and it is not a thing. It is a gift and a skill. It is a gift that another provides; it is a skill that must be exercised by each person within the learned limits of reality. If we would understand freedom, we must be taught; if we would acquire freedom, we must be trained.

Help from a Specialist

I found my best help in doing this in St. Paul's letter to the Galatians. Among the writers of Scripture, Paul is the specialist in matters of freedom. This can be seen in the frequency of Greek words for freedom found in Paul's letters (28 instances) in comparison with the rest of the New Testament (8) and the Apostolic Fathers (6). And in Paul's writings the words for freedom occur more frequently in his letter to the Galatians (10 times) than in any other letter (7 times in Romans; 7 times in 1 Corinthians).

Through the Christian centuries this letter has often been used by God to restore vigor and passion to the life of faith and to confront the world with the realities of a free life in Christ, a life that is free for all: given freely to all of us, making all who receive it free; enabling us to live freely in relation to God and all others. The truth of the Galatian text is documented in the lives of free persons. It *is* possible. The experience is valid. We are not in realms of fantasy. We are not reduced to necessity. Free in Christ, we are free for all.

So I set myself deliberately between Paul's words in Galatians and the words of the people I lived with in church and in the world. I tried to listen in both directions and let the words interact with each other. I pondered and I prayed. I taught and I preached. I encouraged and I directed. I attempted to keep both elements in tension in my imagination and in my ministry—the element of Galatians, churning and surging with the energy of freedom, and the element of people who have given up on freedom and who live apathetically or fatalistically.

I wanted to stay immersed in the complexities of a full life, to accept all the necessities of a responsible life, and still to live freely. This book is an interim report on the continuing work of training and being trained in a way of life developed at God's initiative and in relation to his freedom. It is not biblical exposition or commentary in any classic sense; it is more like prayer—a continuing conversation that searches after understanding, sometimes digressing, but returning again and again to the word of God in the text to listen, to reflect, to answer, and to learn.

The development has not been orderly. Sometimes I am puzzled by Paul, sometimes exasperated by people, sometimes dismayed at my own slowness of heart to believe. I am put in numerous situations, both personal and pastoral, in which I feel there is little or no freedom. There are other times when I am with people who, even while they experience the entrapments that life springs on them, still go their way with a light step and graceful mien. Every time this happens it is a marvel. Together, over a period of years, we experience the detailed rightness of what it means to live as free persons, traveling light.

Some things became clear very early. For one thing, all the rah-rah formulas of freedom that our society spawns are nonsense. They are either simplistic, escape-hatch freedoms from responsibility or vulgar, manipulative freedoms to exploit others. Many people have tried one or more of them, found them unworkable or immoral, and, hearing of no other freedom, succumbed to "lives of quiet desperation."[2]

It also became clear that there are no absolute freedoms. Absolute freedoms are fantasy freedoms. They deny God and they ignore creation, using only the ego as a base for freedom. They brook no qualification, no limitation, no compromise, no relationship. They do not grow out of wise and artful dealing with the human condition, but rather, severed from the actual, they float colorfully and aimlessly in the air like helium-filled party balloons. "The first condition of freedom," say Will and Ariel Durant, "is its limitation; make it absolute and it dies in chaos."[3]

Pioneers of the Free Spirit

I, for one, do not underestimate the difficulties in living free for all, of traveling light: it is persistently hard. Nor can I do it on my own: I need Christ and a community of faith. But there is nothing more worthwhile doing. Many Christians today have to all appearances ceased to be what Jacques Ellul calls "unconscious revolutionaries."[4] It is necessary to rouse awareness, to waken the spirit, because freedom is essential if all would be truly human. I am convinced that people settle for far too little in matters of freedom. Christians, in touch with the God who grants us a freedom far richer than its political and cultural versions, are in the privileged but awesomely responsible position of pioneers of the free spirit, the free life. Nicolas Berdyaev insists: "God has laid upon man the duty of being free, of safeguarding freedom of spirit, no matter how difficult that may be, or how much sacrifice and suffering it may require."[5]

To discover movements of freedom in oneself where there has been only fear-ridden and cowering subjection; to stimulate a free word or act in persons submerged in apathy or pessimism, sluggishly living out their days with diminishing expectations and dwindling energy—these are gloriously worth doing.

Paul an apostle—not from men nor through man, but through Jesus Christ and God the Father, who raised him from the dead—and all the brethren who are with me,

To the churches of Galatia:

Grace to you and peace from God the Father and our Lord Jesus Christ, who gave himself for our sins to deliver us from the present evil age, according to the will of our God and Father; to whom be the glory for ever and ever. Amen.

Galatians 1:1-5

2 Free to Live

A WEALTHY TEXAN WAS being buried in style. According to the instructions written in his will, he was propped behind the wheel of his solid gold Cadillac. The car was poised before a large grave excavated in the prairie. On signal, the brakes were released and the lavish automobile, with its erstwhile owner, rolled gently down the incline into the grave. As it drifted to a stop and the dust settled, one spectator said in awe, "Man, that's livin'!"

A rather poor joke, but a telling parable. The punch line is repeated—with no sense of irony, no awareness of jest—frequently, far too frequently, in everyday life. In 1978 all my friends were telling me that I simply must see the museum exhibit of the treasures of King Tutankhamen. Everyone was going. Long lines of people were crowding their way to see the splendid display. I fully intended to join them but was prevented. I had to depend on reports and photographs. What I remember most about the reports were sophisticated variations on the phrase "Man, that's livin'!" It dawned on me one day that people were talking about a corpse and a tomb. The gold was so *alive,* my friends said. The jewelry communicated such a sense of *vitality.* Then another contrast took shape in my imagination: between that treasure-packed Egyptian tomb and an empty tomb in Palestine. And I thought about how the source of life for persons, who, now and for centuries past, have crowded weekly into churches all over the world, came from the empty tomb from which no jewelry, no artifacts and no corpse had been recovered. Out of that emptiness poured the freedom to live.

A Story of Life and Death
On the first page of the Bible we read that God creates life; two pages later man and woman choose death. History narrates the antiphony between God's will to life and the human will to death.

The word *life,* in the Bible and in all deeply imagined literature, means far more than biological existence. The word *death,* likewise, means far more than the termination of biological function. Each word is rich in both literal and metaphorical nuance. Using the words in these deep and penetrating ways, the Bible tells the story of the life of God and of the death of persons.

Keen observers of the human condition support the biblical declaration that in all the essentials that have to do with its created being, the human is dead. The testimony is well documented in all cultures across many centuries. Whether these observers believe in God or not, they can see that there is something ultimately wrong with the condition in which persons find themselves. Genesis reports God's saying, "You shall not eat of the fruit of the tree which is in the midst of the garden . . . lest you die" (Gen 3:3).

The fruit was eaten. The story continues, but insofar as it is a story about men and women and not of God, it is a story of death. In our day Samuel Beckett, who does not believe in God, accepts God's description of the human condition, witnessing in curt despair, "Man is a terminal illness."[1]

Genesis and Beckett are strange bedfellows, but bedfellows nonetheless. The ancient Hebrew theologian and the modern Irish dramatist agree: if there is a story of persons to be told, it is a story of death. "You shall die" (Gen 2:17); "man is a terminal illness"(Beckett).

So when Paul refers to persons as dead through trespasses and sins (Eph. 2:1), he can in no way be supposed to be mordantly eccentric; he expresses the assured results of what was realized by the ancients and has been confirmed by the moderns. And when he passionately cries out, "Who will deliver me from this body of death?" (Rom 7:24), he cannot be accused of hysterical melodrama—his anguish is common to all who have honestly confronted the human condition. The pre-Christian sage (the author of Genesis), the Christian convert (Paul) and the post-Christian nihilist (Beckett) agree in this at least: the story of humanity is a story of death.

The story of freedom then cannot begin with an analysis of humankind, with a search into the cell or the soul or the mind. Freedom cannot be discovered in a corpse, no matter how close or sympathetic the study, no matter how technically sophisticated the instruments of examination. The most honest and searching examinations of freedom that begin with the human conclude, rightly, that there is no freedom. There is only economic determinism (Marx), or biological determinism (Freud), or psychological determinism (B. F. Skinner), or philosophical nihilism (Nietzsche). If there is a story of freedom to be told, the story must begin with God. That is what the biblical story does. It does not sentimentally describe a corpse, but vigorously proclaims the God of life. The Bible is not a script for a funeral service, but the record of the proclaimed and witnessed God bringing new life to the dead. Everywhere it is a story of resurrection—life where we expect death. Because of God's word and act, and only because of God's word and act, persons are free to live. But if we begin with the human, there can be no story of freedom, only the analysis of a decaying cadaver. It is no surprise, then, to find that Paul begins his reveille on freedom by trumpeting God's initiating action.

I, Paul, and my companions in faith here, greet the Galatian churches. My authority for writing to you does not come from any popular vote from the people, nor does it come through the appointment of some human higher-up. It comes directly from Jesus Christ and God the Father who raised him from the dead: I'm God-commissioned. So I greet you with the great words: Grace and peace! We know the meaning of those words because Jesus Christ rescued us from the present mess we are in by offering himself as a sacrifice for our sins. God's plan is that we all experience that rescue. Glory to God forever! Amen.

The Story of Freedom

In the story of freedom, God is always the subject; the human, always the object. If men and women are to live free, it will be because of God's actions, not because of our own will or disposition or politics or intelligence. Three paradigmatic instances in Paul's opening lines show God to be subject and the human to be object. Paul is *made* an apostle by God. Jesus is *raised* from the dead by God. We are *rescued* from the present evil age by God. Something is done to us or for us before we do anything. We are acted on before we act. Life is not natural to us; it is supernaturally provided for us. Human freedom to live results from God-initiated resurrection.

No one is born free. Our common human experience prepares us to receive this revealed truth; for when we leave the warm security of the womb, we are immediately embraced in protecting and nurturing arms. If we were set free then, we would merely die. Hunger and thirst, weather and disease, accidents and animals would make short work of us if we were set free. An infant is not born into freedom, but into a network of security and care. If the infant is care*free* it is because of the constant attendance of many who are care*ful*. We begin our lives in an intricate arrangement of constraints, limits, boundaries and restrictions. No one counts that bad. Everyone, in fact, agrees that it is good. But it is not free. If we have nostaligic longings for those years of golden innocence, they are longings not for freedom but for security. We are, if we are fortunate, born secure; we are not born free. We are, however, born with a destiny to freedom and a capacity for freedom which are realized in a life of faith.

Freedom, if we get it, is a deliverance. Every person's growth from infancy through childhood and adolescence to adulthood shows the complexity of the process. Freedom is the result of years of learning, of negotiation, of trial and error, of accident and healing, of venture and failure. It involves the lives of many—not only the person but parents, not only peers but superiors. We cannot be free naturally and on our own; freedom requires permissions, demands, struggles, sufferings, risks.

If freedom were natural, it would be inevitable. But it is not inevitable. Not all lives are free. Many persons do not experience freedom at all as they go from childhood to adulthood; they only exchange determinisms. Dependency on parent is exchanged for dependency on a spouse. Addiction to the breast is exchanged for addiction to alcohol or drugs. The fear of parental authority is exchanged for the fear of peer disapproval. Anxiety over losing the securities of the familiar is exchanged for anxieties that provoke paralysis in face of any change or danger. Spontaneities never occur. Motives never develop. Dreams are never accepted; challenges, never met.

Also, if freedom were natural, it would show itself as the product of a smoothly developing process, the natural unfolding of bud to blossom, instead of what it is in fact, a victorious prize in pitched battle. Our freedom to live does not come out of quiet Sunday afternoon reveries in meadows fragrant with rose of Sharon and Easter lily, but out of the dark, dramatic agonies marked by Lucifer's plunge from the heights and war in heaven, cries for crucifixion and the dread *"Eloi, Eloi, lama sabachthani?"* The story of freedom is like that of the earth's crust. Exposed cross sections of the earth tell of volcanic eruptions, violent earthquakes, devastating droughts and ravaging floods, intermixed with strata showing stretches of quietness and mild calm. Signs of ice-age austerities alternate with evidence of tropical lushness. The present free moment in any person's life is not a natural accumulation of goodness, but a paragraph in a history of conflict comprising alienation and reconciliation, advance and retreat, war and peace. The verbs of freedom are *made, raised, rescued.* And God is the subject of each of them.

This Present Evil Age
Paul describes the course of the world apart from Christ as "this present evil age." Any people who attempt to live in defiance of God—and every age makes the attempt—lives badly. Sin destroys our capacity to live. It weakens our vitality. It blinds us to truth. It incapacitates us for living out a healthy love and a vigorous peace. We need deliverance from it. God provides deliverance from it, decade after decade, generation after generation, "according to the will of our God and Father." That is the promise

of the gospel. That is the experience of the Christian. That is the theme of the Galatian letter.

"This present evil age." We are born into a world that shows everywhere the signs of some great primordial catastrophe. There are vast beauties and breathtaking virtues in this present age, but nothing pristine. The sign of our birth is a scar. The world into which we are born is dangerous. The parents to whom we are born are flawed. The governments under which we are reared are corrupt. Are we free to live? Or are we only allowed a meager energy and a compromised space to cope?

Sin is the fact of separation from God's presence and purposes, experienced variously as restriction, limitation, inadequacy and weakness. Every interruption of the will or impulse or desire interferes with freedom. And the interruptions are endless. Life lived under these conditions cannot be called free, even though there will always be unforced and spontaneous moments that preserve a sense of the possibilities of freedom. Sensitive and thoughtful persons are often acutely aware of enslavement. Paul's explosive "Who will deliver me from this body of death?" (Rom 7:24) is archetypal.

It is God's will "to deliver us from the present evil age." Freedom begins here at the point of rescue. Martin Luther found the entire epistle compressed into this phrase.[2] Christ's death and resurrection constitute a rescue from the enslavement to "this present evil age" in which there is no access to the future, to relationships, to God. The key word *deliver (exaireō)* "denotes not a removal from, but a rescue from the power of."[3] The emphasis of the word is upon the act of rescue.

The word must be read closely here, and in context. The rescue is not from the world, and not from limitations or boundaries, but from sin, that which separates us from God and his purposed creation and destined redemption.

And the rescue is God's work. Nothing else will do for a beginning. If there is no rescue from sin, there is no point in talking about freedom at all.

The Christian memory is well stocked with recollections of this deliverance. Early Christian preaching rehearsed the evidence. Stephen, in his famous sermon, remembered Joseph, sold into Egypt " . . . but God was with him, and rescued [*exaireō*] him out of all his afflictions, and gave him favor and wisdom before Pharaoh, king of Egypt, who made him governor over Egypt" (Acts 7:9-10). Now Joseph was a man who, participating in the will of God for deliverance, multiplied the consequences of deliverance and spread them out over an entire generation. He made a difference. Remembering the Joseph story, we realize that no pit or prison is inaccessible to the freeing, delivering, rescuing power of God, and that freedom, once established even in one person, extends itself into political and social relationships and cultural movements.

Over a thousand years later, in the early days of the church, King Herod "laid violent hands upon some who belonged to the church" (Acts 12:1). He killed James and put Peter, the leader of the small Christian band, in prison. Herod found that his action pleased many. He was a man who made decisions on the grounds of what would get him the most applause, a not uncommon characteristic in so-called leaders.

That would put a stop to the hymn-singing Christians! *That* would show the people where the center of power was. *That* would show these people who prattled about freedom the tough realities of the world. But in the middle of the night Peter was delivered from the prison. Out in the street Peter said, "Now I am sure that the Lord has sent his angel and rescued *(exaireō)* me from the hand of Herod and from all that the Jewish people were expecting" (Acts 12:11).

What were the people expecting? The people were expecting the extermination of this one bright hope. The people were expecting that Roman power would crush anyone that stepped out of line. The people were expecting more oppression and more taxes. They didn't believe that there was freedom to believe and sing. They didn't believe that God could change things. They didn't believe that a life of faith could make a difference. And so they grimly and joylessly allied themselves with the forces of society, the culture, the age. They concluded that there was no use going against the grain of "this present evil age," and so they supported Herod over against Peter. But Peter was set free, and shortly afterwards Herod was a diseased corpse (Acts 12:23).

Paul's word *delivered (exaireō)* is not rhetoric, not propaganda, nor cheerleading. It is history: documented deliverance.

The Free Spirit

The rescue was not only remembered; it was personally experienced. F. F. Bruce describes Paul as the "apostle of the free spirit."[4] Paul himself experienced what he preached and taught and wrote. Three phrases in the opening paragraph of Galatians are windows into Paul's experience of rescue which launched him into a life of freedom. First, he calls himself an apostle: "Paul, an apostle . . ." An apostle is a person invited by Christ to be with him and then sent out to represent his gospel, declaring the meaning of his life and death and resurrection, inviting others to receive that life by faith. That is Paul's identity: everything he did and spoke and wrote was a result of being with Christ and being sent out by Christ. The free life was not a genetic endowment but a divine assignment. He had nothing of his own to say, no good works of his own to practice. He was an authorized and commissioned representative of his Lord. Kierkegaard once distinguished between a genius and an apostle by saying that the genius impresses us with his own brilliance, the apostle with God's glory.

A second detail in Paul's experience of freedom is described in the phrase "not from men nor through man, but through Jesus Christ and God the Father, who raised him from the dead." This life of freedom was not formed out of parental influences in his Jewish home. Nor was it a product of his rabbinical education under the famous Jerusalem scholar Gamaliel. Nor did geography or politics have anything to do with it—he doesn't refer to himself as a Roman citizen from Tarsus. He knew himself as shaped and guided, created and redeemed by God through Jesus Christ. (A few years ago I saw an oriental college student wearing a T-shirt with the lettering, "Made in Japan." It was amusing, but it was wrong. None of us are made by our nation, or by our race, or by our parents. We are not made in America. And we certainly are not self-made.) Paul's self-understanding is accurate and profound: we get to the essentials of freedom, not in terms of psychology or culture, but in terms of sin and grace, creation and salvation, judgment and redemption as these are revealed fully in Jesus Christ.

The third phrase that bears on Paul's sense of freedom is "all the brethren who are with me." Paul is free in the context of community. He is not a lonely, solitary, spiritual giant who towers over other Christians and condescendingly consents to straighten them out when they go wrong. He is not free from the failings and demands and troubles of others. He is free *with* them. He is one of them. He is always aware and grateful for the "brethren who are with me." Being immersed in the community doesn't suppress or stifle any of Paul's unique freedom. What he writes has no appearance of a committee report—the whole letter churns and cascades. "It is not a treatise but a sword-cut in a battle, dealt, in an hour of great peril, by a combatant facing formidable foes."[5] So it is clear that the community in no way inhibits or compromises Paul's freedom; it is an aspect of freedom, a support and encouragement to it. Except for Jesus, Paul was the most original and creative individual to live in the first century, and yet he was deeply and humbly involved in a nurturing community of persons. What a contrast that is to the proud, isolated succession of first-century caesars whose names are now only entries in history books. We never develop the freedoms of maturity and wholeness and strength on our own, but always through the shared life of others in the faith.

Withdrawal from Freedom
The age is evil. We fear nuclear holocaust, overpopulation, destruction of the ozone layer, starvation in the third world and double-digit inflation, along with assorted personal fears of rejection and failure, insignificance and ill health. Fear is a normal response to the chaos around us, the threat of being overcome by hostile forces or of being ineffective or hurt or thwarted or fated to poor and mean and scrubby lives. These fears are fed by the news of the day, the predictions of pundits and the disorder of our own emotions.

It is little wonder that people overwhelmed by such fears seek escape from this present evil age by withdrawing from it, by reducing their hope, by avoiding what they cannot control or understand. It is far easier to huddle in self-pity or whine in resentment or gossip rumors of doomsday than submit to rescue. It takes a certain bold courage to receive freedom. The free life is a strenuous life. Living in freedom is demanding and sometimes painful. If security is our highest priority, we will not want to live free. Erich Fromm's book *Escape from Freedom* traces the elaborate attempts by which people avoid the freedom that is given to them, preferring to exist in the secure slaveries provided by totalitarian governments, or totalitarian habits, or totalitarian emotions, or totalitarian addictions.[6]

In every generation great crowds of people mindlessly shuffle along with the herd and do nothing beyond providing statistics for sociological surveys. But also in every generation a few persons live intelligently and courageously in freedom, For these persons, the letter to the Galatians has often been the catalyst to the free life. At several critical times in history this letter, listened to by small groups of Christians, has shifted the direction of the age just enough to make the difference between a surge of new life and a drifting into decline. When people have felt victimized by fear and oppression, it has been a means of setting them free. When many have been paralyzed by anxiety and apprehension, it has stimulated them to an energetic hope. When there has been widespread confusion and bickering and uncertainty about what life was, it has clarified and convinced people of exactly what it means to live openly and well, convinced them to the point of participation in the rescue by which God sets us free to live.

Paul's greeting anticipates what we can expect: "grace . . . and peace." Grace! Life is a gift. Peace! Life is whole. The two words declare that we are, fundamentally and finally, free to live. Life is what we are given, not what we salvage out of the ruins of home and culture. Life is an entirety into which we grow, not a fragment that we snatch on the run.

I am astonished that you are so quickly deserting him who called you in the grace of Christ and turning to a different gospel—not that there is another gospel, but there are some who trouble you and want to pervert the gospel of Christ. But even if we, or an angel from heaven, should preach to you a gospel contrary to that which we preached to you, let him be accursed. As we have said before, so now I say again, If any one is preaching to you a gospel contrary to that which you received, let him be accursed.

Am I now seeking the favor of men, or of God? Or am I trying to please men? If I were still pleasing men, I should not be a servant of Christ.

For I would have you know, brethren, that the gospel which was preached by me is not man's gospel. For I did not receive it from man, nor was I taught it, but it came through a revelation of Jesus Christ.

Galatians 1:6-12

---

3 Free to Curse

Cursing, before it degenerated into mere profanity, was noble religious speech. Genesis records the first curses: the serpent cursed to eat dust, woman cursed with pain in childbirth, man cursed with toil, the ground cursed with thorns and thistles. Curses express God's displeasure with the misuse of freedom and decree consequences that make the misuse unprofitable.

An impressive scene in Deuteronomy shows Israel, rescued from Egyptian slavery and thoroughly trained for a life of freedom, assembled in the new land of Canaan on the mountains Ebel and Gerizim with the Levites thundering curses that will follow the abuse of freedom and singing blessings that will accompany its proper use.

Paul continues the venerable practice and pronounces a vigorous double curse on persons who pervert the life of gospel freedom.

I can't believe your fickleness—how easily you have turned traitor to him who called you by the grace of Christ to a variant gospel! It is not a minor variation, you know; it is completely other, an alien gospel, a no-gospel, a lie about God. Those who are provoking this agitation among you are turning the gospel of Christ on its head. Let me be blunt: if we—even if an angel from heaven!—were to preach something other than what we preached originally, let him be cursed. I said it once; I'll say it again: If anyone, regardless of reputation or credentials, preaches something other than what you received originally, let him be cursed. Do you think I speak this strongly in order to manipulate crowds? or curry favor with God? or get popular applause? If my goal was popularity I wouldn't bother being Christ's slave. Know this—I am most emphatic here, friends—this good news that I have proclaimed to you is not mere human optimism. I didn't receive it through the traditions, and I wasn't taught it in school: I know it through a revelation of Jesus Christ.

Tolerating Heresy

Paul is angry. He is not mildly indignant; he is furious. "Hot indignation seizes me" (Ps 119:53). He is angry over what many would count a small thing, a mere matter of a lie about God. Why be so upset? It can't make much difference. What difference does it make what somebody says about God? It is the way we live that counts.

With Paul's anger as precedent, the church, for much of its life, has held that a lie about God, commonly called a "heresy," is a great and terrible evil. People nowadays think such indignation bad mannered, if not barbaric. Burning people at the stake because they hold to an idea that isn't approved by the bishop is the farthest thing from "civilized." We condemn our forbears as intolerant. We accuse them of bigotry. If we understood, though, what they were doing, we might appreciate their concern even if we did not approve their program. The word *heresy* comes from the Greek word meaning "choose." The heretic is a person who chooses a single item out of the entire body of truth and, ignoring or denying the rest of it, makes that privately preferred and chosen truth the only truth, and teaches others to do the same. Heresy is the choice of a fraction instead of the integer. Insofar as the heretic gets others to see only that fragment and ignore the rest, he blocks access to the organic fullness of all reality, of God. There is simplification in that choice (that is the attraction), but there is also immense impoverishment. The heretic solves our problems by reducing our lives.[1]

We have never before faced so many heretics, and the quality of our lives has never been so bad, which is evidence that far too many people are getting their view of reality from heretics. Today's heretics are well educated, glamorous, persuasive and insistent. We are appalled that the church once burned heretics. Now we make celebrities of them and reward them with six-figure salaries. It was certainly a moral disaster on the part of our ancestors when they got rid of heretics by burning them, but it is metaphysical stupidity on our part to applaud their lies. Our forebears at least knew that something was wrong that had to be contested; our age is so biblically illiterate that it will accept anything provided it is spoken with evident sincerity and accompanied by a big smile.

Our age has developed a kind of loose geniality about what people say they believe. We are especially tolerant in matters of religion. But much of the vaunted tolerance is only indifference. We don't care because we don't think it matters. My tolerance disappears quickly if a person's belief interferes with my life. I am not tolerant of persons who believe that they have as much right to my possessions as I do and proceed to help themselves. I am not tolerant of nations that believe my government is oppressive and corrupt and proceed to make the world better by subverting or attacking my country. I am not tolerant of businesses that believe that their only obligation is to make a profit and that pollute our environment and deliver poorly made products in the process. And Paul is not tolerant when people he loves are being told lies about God, because he knows that such lies will reduce their lives, impair the vitality of their spirits, imprison them in old guilts, and cripple them with anxieties and fears.

Lies about God

We can tell just how angry Paul was by the way he writes. All Paul's other letters follow a certain stylized form. He begins with a greeting and then gives thanks for the persons to whom he is writing. First the greeting, then the gratitude. Invariably. Primary in Paul's heart is gratefulness for his friends, gratitude for what God has done in them, a sense of blessing in knowing them and sharing the life of Christ with them. Every letter he writes follows this pattern—with one exception. When he writes to the Galatians he is so irate and upset that he forgets the thanksgiving. Where we expect to read "I thank God for you . . ." we read "I am astonished that you are so quickly deserting him who called you in the grace of Christ and turning to a different gospel." Then he unloads a double curse on certain persons who were preaching a "gospel contrary," that is, lying about God. These lies were ruining the Galatians' newly experienced free life in Christ: "Let him be accursed. . . . Let him be accursed" *(anathema estō)*.[2] "Here riseth a question, whether it be lawful for Christians to curse?" asks Luther. "Why not? Howbeit not always, nor for every cause."[3]

Vince Lombardi, one of the greatest coaches of this century, yelled angrily at one of his players, "Caffery, if you cheat in a practice session, you will cheat in a game." This is where most coaches would stop. But Lombardi went

on, "And if you cheat in a game, you will cheat for the rest
of your life, and I will not have it."[4] That is Paul's position:
a lie about God becomes a lie about life, and he will not
have it. Nothing counts more in the way we live than what
we believe about God. A failure to get it right in our minds
becomes a failure to get it right in our lives. A wrong idea
of God translates into sloppiness and cowardice, fearful
minds and sickly emotions.

One of the wickedest things one person can do to others
is to lie to them about God, to represent God as other or less
than he is. It is wicked to tell a person that God is an angry
tyrant storming through the heavens, out to get every tres-
passer and throw him into the lake of fire. It is wicked to
tell a person that God is a senile grandfather dozing in a
celestial rocking chair with only the shortest of attention
spans for what is going on in the world. It is wicked to tell
a person that God is a compulsively efficient and utterly
humorless manager of a tightly run cosmos, obsessed with
getting the highest productivity possible out of history
and with absolutely no concern for persons apart from their
usefulness.

If we believe that God is an angry tyrant, we are going to
defensively avoid him if we can. If we believe that God is
a senile grandfather, we are going to live carelessly and
trivially with no sense of transcendent purpose. If we believe that God is an efficiency expert, we are going to live
angry at being reduced to a function and never appreci-
ated as a person.

It is wicked to tell a person a lie about God because, if
we come to believe the wrong things about God, we will
think the wrong things about ourselves, and we will live
meanly or badly. Telling a person a lie about God distorts
reality, perverts life and damages all the processes of living.

Paul at one time had believed "the gospel contrary," the
lie about God. He had a wrong idea of God and from the

basis of that wrong idea was launched on a career of imprisoning and killing the people who didn't share his wrong
idea. He was the scourge of the church. His fine intelligence, immense energy and moral fervor made him a person to be reckoned with. All this was put to the task of hate
and persecution—*religious* hate and persecution.

Not that Paul was, in himself, a hate-filled person. But
he had been told the lie that God was against everyone
who deviated from a certain path. He believed the lie and
so he also was against everyone who didn't follow the path.
As he lived out this lie, he became obsessed.

Paul's idea of God was that he was an angry bachelor
uncle, impatient with the antics of romping and undisci-
plined children. Paul's response, along with many others,
was to shut up the children and make them sit in a corner
until they learned to behave in such a way that they wouldn't
disturb the old man, and if they wouldn't shut up, send
them off to boarding school.

Then he was shown the truth about God. Until this revelation he had simply taken what others told him about God
and worked with that. Now Paul discovered a personal relationship with God himself—no more secondhand rumor
but firsthand faith. He immediately knew that God was
not what he had been told at all—that was all a lie. God
was not *against* but *for*. God was not furious but compassionate. God was not out to get sinners so that he could make
them good and sorry; he was out to get sinners so that he
could make them good and joyful. This truth about God
came to Paul in the person of God's son, Jesus Christ. Jesus
Christ showed him that he had had it all wrong, that what
he had followed was a "gospel contrary." He convinced him
that God is on our side; he persuaded him that sin is not
God's excuse to get rid of us, but the occasion for entering
into our lives and setting us free.

When Paul realized this truth about God and experienced the new way of life that developed out of it, he embarked on a series of arduous journeys to tell others what he had learned and experienced. He didn't want anyone to go on living on lies about God. He knew that if a person had the wrong idea about God, he would have the wrong idea about life. And he would not have it.

Good News

Paul had a favorite word for this great, all-encompassing truth about God: *gospel.* Good news. *Euangellion.* In the writings we have of his, he uses the word sixty times. (Mark used the word only seven times; Matthew, four times; Luke, twice; and John, once.)

He learned the word from Isaiah. That greatest preacher of Israel introduced the word as he addressed a people who were sunk in the deepest kind of gloom. The people had just survived a colossal disaster and were now a conquered people in exile. They were cut off from their traditions. They were the laughingstock of the world community, humiliated and mocked. Then Isaiah spoke his word; the life of faith was created anew. Any time we look into the newspapers, or into our own hearts, and despair, we do well to remember that God's people have faced similar prospects, similar reversals, similar headlines, similar assaults on faith, and have recovered from the doubt, been rescued from the pessimism and foreboding, and gone on to live in praise of God.

Isaiah's sermon was the turning point for those people. "Comfort, comfort my people, says your God. Speak tenderly to Jerusalem, and cry to her that her warfare is ended, that her iniquity is pardoned. . . . Get you up to a high mountain, O Zion, herald of good tidings [gospel!]; lift up your voice with strength, O Jerusalem, herald of good tidings [gospel!], lift it up, fear not; say to the cities of Judah, 'Behold your God!' " (Is 40:1-2, 9-10).

Good tidings. Good news. Gospel. As Paul looks for
the word that will summarize what he wants to say about
God, Isaiah's six-hundred-year-old sermon rushes into
his mind, and the word gospel is there to be used. But this
gospel is not just any good news—not the good news of a
pay raise, or of a good grade in school, or of the victory
of our favorite athletic team, or of the happy solution to
some international problem. It is the unexpected, fresh,
surprising good news that God is not angry or indifferent
or impersonal, but that God loves us and has provided the
means for our salvation. *That* love and *that* salvation are at
the center of absolutely everything, and from that center all
of life is lived. This word has nothing to do with the hope-
ful, brave, encouraging words we use to bolster each other
through hard times and cheer one another on; it is good
news about *God.*

This good news drives out the bad news every time. What
bad news? Anything we name: corrupt Babylon, the unre-
sponsiveness of giant bureaucracies, the taunts of Ishtar's
priests greedily sucking the economy dry, the anger we feel
when the weak and poor are exploited and oppressed, the
despair we experience when we fail in love, the arbitrary
policies of Nebuchadnezzar, the diagnosis that a cancer is
inoperable, the irrational fanaticism of modern dictatorships. William James confidently said that religion will
always drive irreligion to the wall. None of the things we
fear or suffer are untrue, but none has the power to center
our lives, or dominate our emotions, or control our destiny.
God does that. Anyone who tells us something different
is lying to us.

Political and Personal Dimensions
In its biblical usage the word *gospel,* good news, has both
a political and a personal dimension. The political dimension of gospel is good news about the world. In the dazzling

pyrotechnics of world politics we often feel overwhelmed and reduced into insignificance. When we see how easily the daily routines of millions of people can be disrupted by vast impersonal structures, we perceive that as bad news. When we can find no evidence of rationality or morality in world affairs, we know that we live in a world of bad news. No matter how lovely the sunsets, how exquisite the flowers, how haunting the melodies, we are ready to turn to another gospel, a gospel contrary.

Someone says, "You can see for yourself that God is angry. Every headline shows that he is on the rampage. The world is doomed. But, if you will do exactly as I say, I can show you how you can avoid his wrath—but you are going to have to live very carefully and be very, very good."

Scared out of our wits, we listen. Then we hear Paul's indignant, "I am astonished that you are so quickly deserting him who called you in the grace of Christ." We look over the evidence again: Isaiah's Babylon. Paul's Galatia. Our America. Are they so different? Rapacious armies, impersonal bureaucracies, political corruption—"the peoples plot in vain . . . [but] he who sits in the heavens laughs" (Ps 2:1, 4). All the actions of nations and world leaders are performed within a context of God's redemption.

God is cosmic and sovereign. God has the first word and the last. "The kingdom of God is at hand." "Do not fear." History shows that people who believe and live in response to the good news are not naive innocents, but the most clearsighted realists. We are recalled to freedom. We will not abandon the free life of the gospel. Let the people who tell us those lies about God be cursed!

The personal dimension of the gospel is good news about ourselves. The reality of what is within us is every bit as important as the news from the political, industrial and scientific centers of the world. Even if world peace were

an accomplished fact and the domestic economy stabi-
lized to everyone's satisfaction, we still must deal with ourselves.

No matter how nice a house we live in, no matter how
well educated we become, no matter how secure we feel
in job or family, no matter how well we manage to provide an appearance of competence and happiness, if we
are filled with anxieties and guilt and hopelessness, we
cannot make it. If we cannot escape the conviction that
we are no good or have no meaning, that is bad news. We
need a sense of integrity and purpose. We need to count,
to mean something, to be important to somebody, to make
a difference.

Someone says, "Listen, God doesn't have time for your
little problems. He is busy in the Middle East right now.
He has bigger fish to fry. If you want something for yourself, you better get it the best way you can: buy this product
and you will be important; wear these clothes and everyone
will realize how distinguished you are; read this book and
the knowledge will set you a cut above the crowd. Take
care of yourself."

That sounds good; we begin to respond. And then we
hear Paul's indignant, "I am astonished that you are so
quickly deserting him who called you in the grace of
Christ." Instinctively, immediately, we know that he is
right. The only good news that will make a difference is
that the living God personally addresses and mercifully
forgives us. He sets things right at the center. That is what
we need, what we want. We determine that we will not
abandon the free life of the gospel and live in the fantasy
dreams that others paint for us and then sell to us for a
fee. We will live forgiven and in faith, not as a parasite on
others, but creatively for others. We will not mope or cringe
or whine. We will praise and venture and make. Let the
people who tell us those lies about God be cursed!

Let Them Be Cursed

There are well-known religious leaders telling us that world conditions are evidence that God is angry. They advise us that the only way for us to escape his anger is to get as far away from the disorder as possible and be as good as we can, like Jack Horner in the corner. That is a lie. Let them be cursed. There are well-publicized celebrities who tell us that God is far too busy to pay any attention to our feelings and hungers and thirsts, and that if we want anything out of life for ourselves, we better get out and grab it. That is a lie. Let them be cursed.

If we believe these lies about God, we will soon be living a lie with our lives. We will be imprisoned in nervous fear, or we will be imprisoned in compulsive selfishness. And Christ will not have it.

This is the commonest misuse of freedom, to choose a few parts of the world and ignore the rest: choose some political fragments, some personal preferences, parts that appeal to us, parts that feed our neurotic fears, parts that support our ill-considered fantasies, parts that we can understand without too much hard thinking, and then treat these fragments of truth as the whole truth, teaching others the same, and rejecting everything else, rejecting God. This is what Paul names "man's gospel." There is great appeal in it. One has the exhilaration of making a clear choice, and the choice is given zest by the accompanying rejection. But freedom is given to us so that we can embrace the whole of reality, not discard most of it and clutch a few fragments. When we misuse freedom by making it nine parts rejection and one part acceptance, we are cursed. We are told that we will not enjoy what we have chosen and in fact will be separated from all that nurtures and loves. When we teach others to do the same, we rob them of wholeness and life.

God's love and our salvation are completely expressed and fully accomplished in Jesus Christ. That is good news.

As we receive him, we live freely and not apprehensively. We live in open praise and not in piggish greed. Our lives are changed from being obsessed with guilt and ridden with fear to being spontaneous and filled with hope. That's good news!

For you have heard of my former life in Judaism, how I persecuted the church of God violently and tried to destroy it; and I advanced in Judaism beyond many of my own age among my people, so extremely zealous was I for the traditions of my fathers. But when he who had set me apart before I was born, and had called me through his grace, was pleased to reveal his Son to me, in order that I might preach him among the Gentiles, I did not confer with flesh and blood, nor did I go up to Jerusalem to those who were apostles before me, but I went away into Arabia; and again I returned to Damascus.

Then after three years I went up to Jerusalem to visit Cephas, and remained with him fifteen days. But I saw none of the other apostles except James the Lord's brother. (In what I am writing to you, before God, I do not lie!) Then I went into the regions of Syria and Cilicia. And I was still not known by sight to the churches of Christ in Judea; they only heard it said, "He who once persecuted us is now preaching the faith he once tried to destroy." And they glorified God because of me.

Galatians 1:13-24

4 Free to Change

EVERY CHRISTIAN STORY is a freedom story. Each tells how a person has been set free from the confines of small ideas, from the chains of what other people think, from the emotional cages of guilt and regret, from the prisons of the self, sin-separated from God. We are free to change. The process of that change is always a good story, but it is never a neat formula.

We would prefer a formula. We would prefer a medically prescribed drug that would free us from the anxieties of our age. We would prefer a psychological incantation that would release us from the accumulated guilt of our past. We would prefer a religious ritual that would preserve us from the world that wobbles and teeters on the brink of holocaust one day, of futility the next. But freedom doesn't come by formula. It is a story that is worked out within all the complexities and ambiguities of the self and of history.

Robert Penn Warren says, "Everybody wants a big solution to everything. For a long time I would stop people in the street and explain to them what made the world change."[1] As he matured he came to distrust what he calls the "one answer system" for dealing with change, for getting us from where we don't want to be to where we do, and developed "almost a pathological flinch . . . from these oversimplifications, as I think of them, of the grinding problems of life and personality."[2] What he learned to do instead was to tell stories.

That is Paul's way. When he tells us that we are free to change, he doesn't give us a formula; he tells his story. Paul's story is remarkable but by no means exceptional. Similar stories are created and lived daily all over the world, and have been ever since the Lord said to Abraham, "Go from your country and your kindred" (Gen 12:1). Each time such a story is told, it adds to the evidence that we live in a world where we are free to change.

Paul's story is told three times in the Acts of the Apostles (9:1-30; 22:1-21; 26:1-23). This Galatian account is the fourth.

I'm sure that you have heard the story of my earlier life when I lived in the Jewish way. In those days I went all out in persecuting God's church and was systematically destroying it. I was so enthusiastic about the traditions of my ancestors that I advanced head and shoulders above my peers in my career. Even then God had designs on me—why, when I was still in my mother's womb he chose and called me by his grace! Now he intervened and revealed his son to me so that I might joyfully tell Gentiles about him. Immediately—without consulting anyone around me and without going up to Jerusalem to confer with those who were apostles long before I was—I got away into the solitude of Arabia. Later I returned to Damascus, but it was three years before I went up to Jerusalem to compare stories with Cephas. We got on so well that I stayed with him for fifteen days! Except for our Lord's brother, James, I saw no other apostles. (I'm telling you the absolute truth in this.) Only then did I begin my ministry in the regions of Syria and Cilicia. After all that time and activity I was still unknown by face among the Christian churches in Judea. There was only the report: "That man who once persecuted us is now preaching the very faith he used to lay waste." Their response was to glorify God because of me.

The Former Life

Five elements in Paul's story are common to the story of every person that becomes free in Christ. The first element is marked by the phrase "my former life in Judaism." Paul was reared in a Jewish home and educated under the famous Jerusalem rabbi Gamaliel. Great heritage; fine education. To that privileged birth and education, Paul brought extraordinary energy and ability. "I advanced in Judaism beyond many of my own age among my people." He didn't presume that because he had a good name and a good education he could coast. He zealously used what he was given. And he used the gifts in the service of what he called "the tradition of my fathers." He was no rebel trying to find an alternate way, no prodigal son out to sow wild oats, no black sheep determined to defy the family expectations. He was excited by and worked within his heritage.

He describes what he did in these words: "I persecuted the church of God violently and tried to destroy it." Paul's religion set him passionately against what he thought to be wrong. He violently opposed what seemed to him to be evil. Paul was consumed with ambition to make the world orderly and people good. If they wouldn't be good on their own, he would force them to be good; if they proved to be absolutely intractable, he would see that they were eliminated.

Religion, for Paul, was a matter of doing things and making things happen. But is that what religion is? "No amount of Oughtnesses," wrote von Hugel, "can be made to take the place of one Isness."[3] Religion is an awareness of God. It is first of all a desire for what God gives us. It is a free and unforced reaching out for the mercy and love that God offers.

In T. H. White's final volume of his story of King Arthur, he refers to Guenever, now an old woman and abbess in a cloister of nuns. Guenever, he says, "never cared for God. She was a good theologian, but that was all."[4] That describes Paul in his "former life in Judaism"—a good theologian but not interested in God. He was too busy using his education, too busy with his religious projects, too involved in imposing his rich cultural heritage and theological expertise on others. He didn't have time for God.

The Great Reversal
The second element in the story is God's revelation: "when he who had set me apart before I was born, and had called me through his grace, was pleased to reveal his Son to me . . ." Here is a complete reversal in Paul's life. Until this time he was a privileged Hebrew with a rabbinic education and an aptitude for religion, well launched on an action-packed career in which he excelled. He was confident, well-born, successful. Suddenly everything is turned around. God is no longer at the periphery but at the center. He is not the one who does things for God; God does things for him. God is not background for the dramatic events in which Paul is the chief actor; God is the central mover and maker, and Paul is the one moved and made.

Paul realized that God's will for him was in action even before he was born. "He who had set me apart before I was born" is a phrase he remembers from God's address to the prophet Jeremiah (Jer 1:5) and hears it now as God's personal word to him. The words can be applied to any of us. We are not a last-minute intrusion on God's attention.

We are not something incidental to God's plan. We are not something that just happened along in the course of certain biological goings-on in the human race. We are, each of us, "set apart." We are *pre*loved by God.

In that revelation Paul knew himself to be called by God's grace. Invited. No one is left to wander through a trackless desert of history or society or culture. Life is not an aimless groping. We are called. "By his grace" means that God does not look around to see who will best suit his purposes and then single them out because he is pretty sure that they will do a good job. It means that God has a capacity so large in love and purpose that he calls us in order to do something for us—to give us something. Grace.

Paul learned that his ideas about God had been completely cockeyed until God was "pleased to reveal his Son to me." What a surprise that was! For Paul knew all about Jesus, a grubby little teacher who spoke with a hayseed Galilean accent, from a family of nobodies, who was so inept as to get caught in a Sadducee-Roman conspiracy which led to his crucifixion. Afterward some unemployed fishermen and hysterical women ran around telling unlikely stories of his resurrection—the kind of thing you might expect from that class of people.

Then God revealed himself in the person of Jesus to Paul. It was as if God said, "Listen, Paul, you have it all wrong. You have good ideas, your theology is intelligent enough, your sincerity is above reproach, but you have it all wrong. You think religion is a matter of knowing things and doing things. It is not. It is a matter of letting God do something for you—letting him love you, letting him save you, letting him bless you, letting him command you. Your part is to look and believe, to pray and obey. For a start I am going to show myself to you in Jesus. In him you will see that what concerns me is being with you, making you whole. In him you will see that I do not force my way, that I do not shout my will. In him you will see that the way in which I conquer evil is by submitting myself to it, receiving it into myself, and in that act—crucifixion —the power of evil is broken and salvation is accomplished. As for the resurrection, examine the evidence and you will see that it is not hysterical rumor, but fact as soberly and reliably reported as anything on this earth can be."

For the first time in his life, Paul was listening, not talking. He was looking, not demonstrating. He was worshiping God, not pushing people around. Until then he had supposed that his Jewish traditions and rabbinical education and considerable intelligence provided him with everything he needed to know about God, and that all that remained was to go out and put it to work. Now he realized that the central reality was not what he knew about God, but what God knew about him and willed for him and showed him and commanded him. *God* was at the center, not Paul. Paul submitted himself to that will of God and agreed to let God work in him; at the same time he quit trying to subject other people to his will, forcing them to fit into what he thought was best for them.

That is the heart of the Christian story. We accept Christ as Lord and Savior. We realize that God is the living center of life and that he has provided the means by which we can live in conscious, glad relationship with him. We live not by what we know, but by trusting in the God who is for us. We live not by moral projects but by obedient faith. The moment we do that we have our first authentic taste of freedom.

It is significant that Paul did not describe this moment by saying "When I decided to be a Christian," but rather by saying "When he . . . was pleased to reveal his Son to me." Conversion is God's work. We cannot command the heavenly vision. We cannot manipulate the divine will. "It is not given to men to make God speak. It is only given to them to live and to think in such a way that, if God's thunder should come, they will not have stopped their ears."[5]

Solitary Retreat

The third element in Paul's story follows: "I did not confer with flesh and blood . . . but I went away into Arabia; and again I returned to Damascus." Arabia was a place of solitary retreat. A meeting with God requires assimilation and reflection. We are not used to living with God at the center; we are not used to living by grace; we are not used to the feelings of forgiveness.

We have been conned by our society into thinking that in ourselves we are not worth much and so must prove we are something by what we wear or what we produce or what kind of impression we make. We have been bullied by our emotions into concluding that if we don't feel happy something is wrong at the core of the universe, that if we don't have what we want when we want it then we are being deprived of our rights, that if we are suffering or feeling pain then God is not doing his job. We all carry within us, often unconsciously, these and similar attitudes from our parents and our peers. They are wrong and perverse but nevertheless influence us powerfully. Then we are introduced to God's truth: we are loved and forgiven. God is real. We are not resented accidents in his beautifully arranged creation but planned children. How do we make the transition from living our habitual guilts and rejections to living the freedom and acceptance which now surrounds us? Arabia is one way—a place to meditate and praise. A time to sink ourselves, without kibbitzing from friends or family or critics, into newfound truths.

A few hours set aside in a quiet room can be Arabia. An hour of worship each Sunday can be Arabia. Seizing times of apartness and solitude, we can explore the meanings of God's love for us, develop the ramifications of God's

forgiveness of us, deepen the sense of God's acceptance
of us. "I did not confer with flesh and blood . . . but I went
away into Arabia." Out of such days and hours new energies flow, and the skills of freedom are worked into our
daily routines.

Thomas Merton knew how essential Arabia is if we are
to incorporate the freedom that is given in conversion into
our everyday routine. His life is a contemporary witness
to the importance of Arabia. He wrote, "The world of men
has forgotten the joys of silence, the peace of solitude which
is necessary, to some extent, for the fulness of human living. . . . If man is constantly exiled from his own home,
locked out of his own spiritual solitude, he ceases to be a
true person. He no longer lives as a man. He is not even
a healthy animal. He becomes a kind of automaton, living
without joy because he has lost all spontaneity. He is no
longer moved from within, but only from outside himself.
He no longer makes decisions for himself, he lets them
be made for him. He no longer acts upon the outside world,
but lets it act upon him. He is propelled through life by a
series of collisions with outside forces. His is no longer the
life of a human being, but the existence of a sentient billiard
ball, a being without purpose and without any deeply valid
response to reality."[6]

Paul was in no hurry to get back to work. He didn't have
to be in a hurry for he knew that God was at work. God
didn't need him; he needed God. Arabia was his place and
time for the leisurely, contemplative training in which he
got used to this new way of life in which God was at the
center, in which he himself was accepted, and in which he
could travel light.

Sharing Our Stories
A fourth element in the story takes place in Jerusalem:
"Then after three years I went up to Jerusalem to visit

Cephas, and remained with him fifteen days." The word "to visit" is, in Greek, *historeō*, the word behind our "history." It has a colloquial tone to it—"to sit down and swap stories." Paul didn't go to Peter to lecture him or to report to him or to propagandize him. He went to visit. The two men put their feet up in front of a few coals of fire and traded stories: "How did God get hold of you, Peter?" "Well, it was a day when I was on the beach on Lake Galilee ..." "And how about you, Paul, tell me your story." And Paul recalled his trauma and ecstasy on the Damascus road.

Every Christian story needs sharing. We require a few other persons to whom we can tell our stories. Every story is different. Every story is the same. How are we to know that what we feel is legitimate and healthy? How are we to know that our story is not a fragment of abnormal psychology? Tell the story. In the telling we recognize the common plot of God's grace setting us apart, personally calling us and revealing his Son to us. We also recognize the great care with which he respects and uses every individual feature of our bodies and emotions and minds so that each story is totally fresh and original.

Paul doesn't exalt his story into a model to which others must conform; he shares it in a conversation with friends who also have stories to tell. In the Jerusalem visit, Peter and Paul become partners instead of rivals. Paul had become a Christian in a very different way from Peter. Peter had been a profane, rough, ungodly person; Paul had been a sophisticated, urbane, pious person. Peter had been converted from a life of sin; Paul, from a life of religion. Peter had been converted in a process of long and intense personal association with Jesus with whom he ate, talked and worked; Paul never saw Jesus personally, but had a brief vision of him along the Damascus road. Peter had the immediate confirmation of the authenticity of his experience by being installed as the leader of the Christian community;

Paul had to live for years with a reputation of being a sadistic killer of Christians.

The fifteen-day visit of Paul with Peter makes plain that no single story is better than another. There is no model conversion. There is no formula in four steps. There is no ritual, whether emotional or liturgical. We are all different. God is the same and has the same salvation to work out in each of us, but he creates an original story every time. We acquire an appreciation for and delight in the individual features of our own stories and of the stories of our friends as we "history" one another in the community of faith.

Sharing *the* Story
A fifth element in Paul's faith story comes before us in the words "I went into the regions of Syria and Cilicia . . . that I might preach him among the Gentiles." The story of faith develops vocational dimensions: Paul has a job to do in the world. He finds ways to say to others what has been said to him—that God is on our side, that God is the one who sets us free to live well, that a living God of love has set apart every one of us in mercy for blessing, that the bonds of sin have been broken and we are free before God.

No life of faith can be lived privately. There must be overflow into the lives of others. The channels of this overflow are numerous and cannot be programmed by one person for another. Paul's life overflowed into the life of missionary to the Gentiles. Others overflow into the life of merchant, or teacher, or salesman, or student, or engineer, or janitor. The channels always open up. The story of faith always opens out into the everyday and takes shape in the world of work, involving other persons in its freely lived love.

Change Me
Randall Jarrall concludes a poem, "Change me, change

me."[7] It is one of the most persistent petitions of the human heart. The petition is answered daily as God sets us free to change and, using the five elements of conversion, begins a new and original story of the free life.

In the story of the changed life, nothing is wasted. Our former lives—in Judaism, in paganism, in secularism, in narcissism—are raw material that is used in the work of art that is freedom. We do not begin to be in relation to God only at the moment we become aware of it. God has had plans for us from before our birth. He has never been apart from us. That which took place in the years before our acceptance of Christ's love is not rejected but used. Nothing is wasted in the free life of faith. Now all is God's. Every word that has truth in it, every thing that is solid is God-originated and God-directed. The change penetrates every part of our selves and our history, not just the "spiritual" parts, not just the good parts. The inferiorities we feel, the inadequacies we sense, the sins we regret, the differences that make us feel like outsiders—these are all included in the story of freedom and are transformed into Christ-affirmed features that express the power and glory of God. As the changes take place we find that we are free to adore, to pray, to believe, to take time to get things right, and to listen again and again for the freedom-creating word.

Then after fourteen years I went up again to Jerusalem with Barnabas, taking Titus along with me. I went up by revelation; and I laid before them (but privately before those who were of repute) the gospel which I preach among the Gentiles, lest somehow I should be running or had run in vain. But even Titus, who was with me, was not compelled to be circumcised, though he was a Greek. But because of false brethren secretly brought in, who slipped in to spy out our freedom which we have in Christ Jesus, that they might bring us into bondage–to them we did not yield submission even for a moment, that the truth of the gospel might be preserved for you. And from those who were reputed to be something (what they were makes no difference to me; God shows no partiality)– those, I say, who were of repute added nothing to me; but on the contrary, when they saw that I had been entrusted with the gospel to the uncircumcised, just as Peter had been entrusted with the gospel to the circumcised (for he who worked through Peter for the mission to the circumcised worked through me also for the Gentiles), and when they perceived the grace that was given to me, James and Cephas and John, who were reputed to be pillars, gave to me and Barnabas the right hand of fellowship, that we should go to the Gentiles and they to the circumcised; only they would have us remember the poor, which very thing I was eager to do.

Galatians 2:1-10

5 Free to Resist

T HE WORD *CHRISTIAN* means different things to different people. To one person it means a stiff, uptight, inflexible way of life, colorless and unbending. To another it means a risky, surprise-filled venture, lived tiptoe at the edge of expectation.

Either of these pictures can be supported with evidence. There are numberless illustrations for either position in congregations all over the world. But if we restrict ourselves to biblical evidence, only the second image can be supported: the image of the person living zestfully, exploring every experience—pain and joy, enigma and insight, fulfillment and frustration—as a dimension of human freedom, searching through each for sense and grace. If we get our information from the biblical material, there is no doubt that the Christian life is a dancing, leaping, daring life.

How then does this other picture get painted in so many imaginations? How does anyone get the life of faith associated with dullness, with caution, with inhibition, with stodginess? We might fairly suppose that a congregation of Christians, well stocked with freedom stories—stories of Abraham, Moses, David, Samson, Deborah, Daniel—would not for a moment countenance any teaching that would suppress freedom. We might reasonably expect that a group of people who from infancy have been told stories of Jesus setting people free and who keep this Jesus at the center of their attention in weekly worship, would be sensitive to any encroachment on their freedom. We might think that a people that has at the very heart of its common experience release from sin's guilt into the Spirit's freedom, a people who no longer lives under the tyranny of emotions or public opinion or bad memories, but freely in hope and in faith and in love—that these people would be critically alert to anyone or anything that would suppress their newly acquired spontaneity.

But in fact the community of faith, the very place where we are most likely to experience the free life, is also the very place where we are in most danger of losing it.

Galatia was an outpost of Christian freedom; it was also surrounded and infiltrated by persons who had a deep antipathy to freedom and had mounted a campaign to squelch it. Paul, guiding the new Christians in the art of preserving their freedom and guarding them from the forces that were hostile to it, tells them of a key experience in his own life when his freedom was on the line.

Fourteen years after that first visit, Barnabas and I went up to Jerusalem and took Titus with us. I went up to clarify with them what had been revealed to me. At that time I placed before them exactly what I was preaching to the Gentiles. I did this in private with the leaders, those held in esteem by the church, so that our concern would not become a controversial public issue, marred by racial tensions and national loyalties, exposing my years of work to denigration and endangering my present ministry. Significantly, Titus, Greek though he was, was not required to be circumcised. While we were in conference we were infiltrated by false brethren who slipped in to spy out the freedom we have in Christ Jesus so that they might reduce us to servitude. We didn't give them the time of day–we were determined to preserve the truth of the gospel for you.

As for those who were held as eminent in the church (their reputation doesn't concern me; God doesn't deal with appearances), they added nothing to my message. On the contrary, they saw that I had been entrusted with the gospel to the Gentiles just as Peter had been to the Jews, for the same one who worked by means of Peter in mission to the Jews was also at work in my ministry to the Gentiles. Now knowing the grace that was given to me, James, Peter and John, the pillars of the church, gave the right hand of fellowship to me and Barnabas, assigning us to a ministry to the Gentiles while they continued to be responsible for the Jews. The only thing they asked was that we remember the poor, and I was already eager to do that.

Freedom Suppressors

Paul locates the source of danger in "false brethren secretly brought in, who slipped in to spy out our freedom which we have in Christ Jesus, that they might bring us into bondage." Why would anyone want to suppress freedom? Why would anyone, once seeing the attractiveness of persons restored to a condition of freedom, do anything to stifle such glory?

For the best of reasons: to protect tradition and to preserve morality. The Jews had a highly developed appreciation for tradition and the finest moral sense of any people in the history of civilization. Freedom was a threat to both tradition and morality. There was always the possibility that a free person would decide to be free *from* tradition and to

live completely immersed in the present. There was always the danger that a free person would disregard moral
wisdom and only accept the trial-and-error results of experience.

Human existence is intricate—physically, psychologically
and socially. It won't do to have everyone doing whatever
each pleases. If all who drive automobiles were given carte
blanche freedom, there would be chaos and carnage. Some
would take shortcuts through flower gardens, some would
choose to drive on whichever side of the highway looked
smoothest, some would stop in the middle of intersections
to gossip with friends. With that kind of freedom, soon no
one would be free: half of us would be snarled in traffic
jams, and the other half hospitalized with broken limbs.

So the anxiety of the people who came in to spy out Paul's
freedom was not irrational. Freedom talk is dangerous
talk. Is it possible to tell people that they are free and expect
that their behavior will coincide with the interests of the
community? Fear of consequences has always been a means
of insuring moral behavior. If fear is replaced by freedom,
will anarchy break loose?

Paul is not unmindful of these dangers, and in his own
time and in his own way (chapters 5—6) he will deal with
them. But he gives his attention to first things first. And
freedom is a first thing.[1] The gospel sets freedom at the
very center of existence. It is not an extra, not an option, not
a superstructure on a foundation of tradition and morality.
It is the foundation.

As Paul tells the Galatians of his Jerusalem experience,
he remembers two areas in which free life in Christ was
challenged: Titus's uncircumcision was challenged and
Paul's ministry to the Gentiles was challenged. Both challenges were met successfully. Paul did not find it necessary
to go along with the forceful currents of the traditionalists
and moralists—he was free to resist.

Free from Preconditions

Titus was a Greek Christian. He had heard the good news that God loved him just as he was. He accepted that news, realized acceptance at the center of his being and lived free. Titus, created by God—his body, his feelings, his thoughts . . . all of these God's gifts. The longings for wholeness, the burdens of sin, the frustrations blocking completeness—all these were met by Christ in a gracious salvation that set him free. He no longer had to take responsibility for every inadequacy; he no longer had to work out and expiate every guilt; he no longer had to master every difficulty; he no longer had to perfect himself as master of his fate. He was simply Titus, set free.

In Jerusalem, though, he was given a thorough going over, spied on and inspected, and told, "No, Titus, you are not free. There is something more basic than God's love for you, something more foundational than Christ's salvation of you."

"Oh," said Titus, "and what could that be?"

"There is circumcision."

"Circumcision? What is circumcision?"

"Circumcision," replied the inspection committee, "is a Jewish ritual that we have been practicing for two thousand years now that provides physical evidence that you are serious about living by faith. It is a simple operation performed on the most private member of your body to show that at the most intimate level of your life you are separated from the world and joined to God. The pain is momentary, but circumcision will be a permanent sign of your faith. Further, it will identify you with the people who have the most extensive and deepest experience with God, the Jewish people. God will not accept you until you accept this condition. God loves you, true; Christ saves you, yes; but you aren't thoroughly accepted until you begin at the beginning, the way every Jew begins, with circumcision."

Why do we keep on doing this to one another? Why do we keep trying to impose some condition or other as prerequisite to God's freely given acceptance? Why can we not simply announce and demonstrate that God's acceptance is the freeing, foundational word?

Our partial acceptances of one another, our conditional acceptances of one another are, in fact, rejections. Acceptance is a carrot held out to motivate us to conform, not a gift to set us free. "If you will dress this way, or talk this way, or behave this way, or learn this, or accomplish that, you will be accepted as one of us." But, however earnestly and politely these conditions are set forth, they are rejections. We are not accepted as we are: we don't have the proper manners; we don't know the right people; we don't have enough education or training; we bring too many neurotic dependencies with us; we haven't yet proved ourselves productive in society. So we are told to wait; we are placed on probation; we are given a training program to complete.

Insofar as we go along with and fail to challenge these partial, conditional rejections, we do not live freely. How can we be free if we are not free to be ourselves without constantly having to please another? How can we live freely if there is a constant threat of having the door shut in our faces because of something we say or fail to say, because of some inadequacy or failure exposed?

The gospel reverses that process: it begins with acceptance, then, with the rush of freedom into the soul that that brings, the spiritual, moral, responsible life develops. Paul resisted the spies and contested the primacy of circumcision, or any other religious precondition; thus the free life in Christ was preserved.

Free to Serve
The second threat to the free life in Christ came in a chal-

lenge to Paul's ministry to the Gentiles. The principle was well established that ministry was "to the Jew first, also the Greek" (Rom 2:10). Jesus' authority could be invoked for support, "Let the children first be fed, for it is not right to take the children's bread and throw it to the dogs" (Mk 7:27). But Paul wasn't following that line. His ministry didn't exclude Jews, but it was primarily among Gentiles. His freedom to do that was challenged in Jerusalem.

Paul wasn't fitting into the grooves. The grooves of apostleship were quite clear: training with Jesus, empowerment at Pentecost, prayer and fasting in the Jerusalem community out of which particular assignments came. Paul had participated in none of that, and apart from a brief fifteen-day visit with Peter, had stayed clear of the apostle-pillared Jerusalem church. Reports, of course, of his maverick ministry had filtered back. It was difficult to be enthusiastically approving. Now that he was in Jerusalem again, they had their chance to get him into the apostolic grooves.

"Look, Paul, you simply are not free to go off and freelance it among the Gentiles. You have a responsibility to the church as a whole, and the church as a whole is centered here in Jerusalem, and given direction by the pillar apostles, Peter and James and John. You didn't even know Jesus Christ. You never heard him teach; you never observed him heal or exorcise; you didn't go through the agonies of his passion. There is nothing in your life that corresponds to that arduous training in discipleship that we received. How can you presume to go off and preach and teach without adequate training and authority? Your problem is that you have been bitten by wanderlust—you want an excuse to travel and indulge your own ego. And what do you know about Gentiles anyway? You are more Jewish than any of us. Pharisaism is in your blood and bones. You have the best rabbinic training of anyone in the church.

Ever since we heard of your conversion we have been making plans for using your particular gifts. What we want you
to do is to be chairman of the education committee. If we
are going to make any inroads into the Sanhedrin, we must
have someone at home in rabbinic arguments. You are
obviously the person for the job; here is the job description
that we have worked out."

Why do we keep doing that to people? to our children,
our friends, our spouses, our leaders? Why do we think
we know God's strategy for ministry so well that we can
write the script for them? Why do we insist on manipulating
and controlling their lives? When someone begins to live
freely, we lose control over them. We become anxious or
maybe envious. We slip in and spy out their freedom. If
everything can be fit into an organization chart, we feel
more secure. But we also lose one of the freedoms of the
gospel, the freedom to experience love and compassion,
acts of love that my parents never thought of, ways of witness that my peers never ventured. Do we not trust God
to call and direct? Do we not remember that one of the great
freedoms that the gospel releases among us is the freedom
to love and serve originally, apart from precedent? Each
of us is an absolutely unique combination of experience
and intelligence and situation. The way we live out that
uniqueness cannot be assigned by another, no matter how
wise or authoritative. It must be creatively worked out
in our own faith responses in the Spirit.

A good friend was told by his mother from the time he
could remember that from the moment of his birth he
had been set aside for "the Lord's work." His mother meant
by that, and the community in which he grew up understood by that, that he would be a pastor in a particular de-
nomination. As he developed he was thrust into a ministe-
rial role, and to all appearances he had all the aptitudes for
it—an arresting public presence, articulate speech, a love

of Scripture. Everybody thought it was working out won-
derfully—except for one person, the man himself. He
had been programmed and trained and guided from childhood for something that was not right for him. He felt
uneasy in the role; he felt guilty because he didn't fit in.
He was meeting all the expectations of family and congregation, but he was not himself.

Finally, he had the courage to break out of the mold.
It was greatly disappointing to all who knew him. But now
he experienced vocational freedom for the first time. He
didn't cease to be a Christian. The intensity with which
he shared his life of faith in Christ was not diminished in
the least. For twenty years now he has been discovering and
developing quite original and surprising forms of ministry.
It is the "Lord's work," but not at all what his mother had
in mind.

He has Paul to thank for the freedom to do that. Paul
boldly and carefully set before the eminent Jerusalem
leaders his gentile ministry, and won their assent, "the
right hand of fellowship, that we should go to the Gentiles."
There are always some in the church who say that the best
way to express the Christian faith is as a pastor, or missionary, or monk, or nun—or in medicine, or social work, or
educational enterprises. There are always some who know
exactly what another is best suited for. But no one knows
us well enough for that. Each of us has unique gifts, for
which there are no precedents, yet which will be used in
ministry. And we are quite free to resist anyone who tells
us differently.

Free to Show Compassion
Paul and the Jerusalem leaders came to an agreement: any
person was free to be a Christian without first becoming
a Jew; any person was free to develop new forms of Christian ministry. Titus's case established the freedom of sheer

being before God; Paul's case established the freedom to do something original before God. It was not necessary to follow the circumcision pattern; it was not necessary to follow the "Jew first, then Gentile" pattern.

In the process of resisting the pressures to conform to established precedents and protect these basic freedoms of being and doing, there was wholehearted agreement on another matter: "They would have us remember the poor, which very thing I was eager to do."

A freedom that ignores or forgets or despises the poor is a bogus freedom. The poor are powerless to insist on their own rights or to negotiate their needs. The moral structures of Judaism and the organization of the Jerusalem church both made provisions for the care of the poor. Would the freedom of the gentile Christians, untutored in the long moral traditions rooted in Sinai, unconnected with the strong centralized administration of the Jerusalem congregation, have any concern for the helpless and the weak? Peter and James and John needed reassurance; Paul unhesitatingly gave it.

Our attitude toward the poor is still one of the surest tests of the health of our freedom. The moment freedom is used to avoid acts of mercy or help or compassion, it is exposed as a fraud. A free person who finds ways to enhance the lives of the poor demonstrates the truest and most mature freedom. A free person who diminishes the lives of the poor by dealing out ridicule or withholding gifts is himself diminished, is herself diminished.

We are free to resist the pressures to conform to an established formula for being rightly related to God; we are free to resist established precedents for working in God's name; we are not free to dismiss poor people from our awareness, to turn a deaf ear to voices that ask for help, to harbor even the slightest contempt for the failures and rejects in our society.

Remaining Vigilant

There are people who do not want us to be free. They don't want us to be free before God, accepted just as we are by his grace. They don't want us to be free to express our faith originally and creatively in the world. They want to control us; they want to use us for their own purposes. They themselves refuse to live arduously and openly in faith, but huddle together with a few others and try to get a sense of approval by insisting that all look alike, talk alike and act alike, thus validating one another's worth. They try to enlarge their numbers only on the condition that new members act and talk and behave the way they do. These people infiltrate communities of faith "to spy out our freedom which we have in Christ Jesus" and not infrequently find ways to control, restrict and reduce the lives of free Christians. Without being aware of it we become anxious about what others will say about us, obsessively concerned about what others think we should do. We no longer live the good news but anxiously try to memorize and recite the script that someone else has assigned to us. In such an event we may be secure, but we will not be free. We may survive as a religious community, but we will not experience what it means to be human, alive in love and faith, expansive in hope. Conforming and self-congratulatory behavior is not free. But Paul "did not yield submission even for a moment, that the truth of the gospel might be preserved for you." Every free person who benefits from Paul's courage will continue vigilant in the resistance movement he formed.

But when Cephas came to Antioch I opposed him to his face, because he stood condemned. For before certain men came from James, he ate with the Gentiles; but when they came he drew back and separated himself, fearing the circumcision party. And with him the rest of the Jews acted insincerely, so that even Barnabas was carried away by their insincerity. But when I saw that they were not straightforward about the truth of the gospel, I said to Cephas before them all, "If you, though a Jew, live like a Gentile and not like a Jew, how can you compel the Gentiles to live like Jews?" We ourselves, who are Jews by birth and not Gentile sinners, yet who know that a man is not justified by works of the law but through faith in Jesus Christ, even we have believed in Christ Jesus, in order to be justified by faith in Christ, and not by works of the law, because by works of the law shall no one be justified. But if, in our endeavor to be justified in Christ, we ourselves were found to be sinners, is Christ then an agent of sin? Certainly not! But if I build up again those things which I tore down, then I prove myself a transgressor. For I through the law died to the law, that I might live to God. I have been crucified with Christ; it is no longer I who live, but Christ who lives in me; and the life I now live in the flesh I live by faith in the Son of God, who loved me and gave himself for me. I do not nullify the grace of God; for if justification were through the law, then Christ died to no purpose.

Galatians 2:11-21

6 Free to Explore

THE NORWEGIAN DRAMATIST Ibsen tells the story of Peer Gynt going to a mental hospital and surprisedly finding that no one in the place seemed crazy. They all talked so sensibly and discussed their plans with such precision and concern that he felt sure they must be sane. He spoke to the doctor about it. "They're mad," said the doctor. "They talk very sensibly, I admit, but it is all about themselves. They are, in fact, most intelligently obsessed with self. It's self—morning, noon, and night. We can't get away from self here. We lug it along with us, even through our dreams. O yes, young sir, we talk sensibly, but we're mad right enough."[1]

The world is much like the hospital visited by Peer Gynt. It seems sane enough until we realize that it is possessed with itself. All it talks about are its feelings, its politics, its wars, its budgets, its money. The largest part of existence,

God, is unmentioned. Persons who become absorbed in this conversation, who let the world dominate the conversation, who accept the world's definition of values, who respond in knee-jerk fashion to everything that the world calls an emergency, become frightened, anxious, inhibited and demoralized. There is no way to live freely under such conditions. No matter how factual life may seem, no matter how sensibly it is all presented, if it is all done from within the hospital, excluding the people and facts and events outside the hospital, it is crazy all the same.

Christ leads people out of the confines of the world hospital into the open air of God. In the open air things are not as cozy as they are in the hospital. Everything is not labeled. Every person is not defined. When we decide to leave the obsessive self-preoccupations of the world and live in expansive adoration of God, we are plunged into mystery, into growth, into an abundance beyond our abilities to classify or administer. Reality is increased beyond our capacity to manage it; it is not reduced to the cramped dimensions of our greed or lust or covetousness or fear.

Sometimes we are tempted to return to the hospital. And all the time, of course, the hospital's doctors and administrators are trying to get us back in. There are constant appeals to return to the hospital. They need to justify their existence, and so they define us in terms of our sickness. The majority of the people who make claims on us insist that the hospital is the real world.

But once out, we are not returning. We are going to live freely. Who are we, though, to disbelieve such highly credentialed persuaders? Who are we to believe in an invisible God instead of their clearly visible statistics? Who are we to read Galatians as a means of discovering the dimensions of our lives and the meaning of freedom instead of the latest newsletter from the world hospital inviting us to its therapy sessions? We are Christians; that is who we are.

We encourage one another in the strenuous life that nurtures and protects a healthy freedom in faith so that we are not deceived by the surface appearance of sanity in the madhouse of the world. We read Paul's two-thousand-year-old letter to his Galatian friends and are taught how to live freely in God, not in bondage to the world, to live spontaneously, not obsessively.

Continuing the personal reminiscence in which his own freedom was challenged, Paul completes that story and then concludes it with a remarkable summary that is redolent with the open-aired, lung-expanding, spirit-deepening reality in which we explore the elements of the free life, leaving the cramped, stifling, labeled, self-occupied asylum of the world to "live to God."

Later, when Cephas came to Antioch, I had a face-to-face confrontation with him because he was obviously wrong. Earlier, before certain persons had come from James, he regularly ate with the Gentiles, but when they came he cautiously pulled back and put as much distance as he could manage between himself and his gentile friends, so fearful was he of the circumcision clique. Worse, the rest of the Jews in the church joined in that hypocrisy so that even Barnabas was swept along in the charade. But when I saw that they were not maintaining a steady, straight course according to the gospel, I spoke up to Cephas in front of them all, "If you, a Jew, live like a Gentile and not like a Jew when you are not being observed by the spies from Jerusalem, what right do you have to require Gentiles to conform to Jewish customs just to make a favorable impression on your old Jerusalem cronies?"

We, who were born sinners in the Jewish way rather than the gentile, well know that a person is not set right with God by rule keeping but only through personal faith in Jesus Christ. How do we know? We tried it—and we had the best system of rules the world has ever seen. Convinced that no human being can please God by self-improvement, we believed in Jesus Christ so that we might be set right before God by faith in Christ, not by trying to be good.

Have some of you noticed that we are not yet perfect? And are you ready to make the accusation that since people like me, who seek to be justified by Christ, aren't perfectly virtuous, Christ must therefore be an accessory to sin? The accusation is frivolous. If I was "trying to be good," I would be reconstructing the same old barn that I tore down and acting as a charlatan. What actually took place is this: I tried keeping rules and working my head off to please God, and it didn't work; so I quit so that I could simply be, so I could live in harmony with God. Christ's life showed me how and enabled me to do it. I identified myself completely with him; indeed I have been crucified with Christ. My ego is no longer central. It is no longer important that I appear righteous before you or have your good opinion, and I am no longer driven to please God. Christ lives in me: the life you see me living is lived by faith in the son of God who loved me and gave himself for me. I am not going to go back on that. Is it not clear to you that to go back to that old rule-keeping, peer-pleasing religion would be an abandonment of everything personal and free in relationship with God? I refuse to do that, to repudiate God's grace. If a living relationship with God came by rule keeping, then Christ died gratuitously.

Justified by Faith in Christ

Five phrases in this section reflect the open-air reality that breathes new life into the person who has just left the world hospital. Dismissed from the hospital we are free to explore the many dimensions of freedom.

The first phrase is "justified by faith in Christ." Justification means being put together the way we are supposed to be. Made right—not improved, not decorated, not veneered, not patched up, but justified. Our fundamental being is set in right relationship with God.

This setting right is not impersonal fixing; it is personal reconciliation. We are never right in ourselves, but only in response to and as a result of God working in and through us. We can never be justified apart from God, but only in some kind of communion with him.

Therefore we must have faith, for faith is the personal relationship supreme. Justification is not coercive; it is not accomplished impersonally by a committee; it is not brought about politically by government legislation or edict; it is not done by a social program financed through taxes or a church program financed through a philanthropist. It comes by faith, the willing responsiveness and involvement of a free person.

This faith through which we participate in justification is voluntary, but it cannot (and this is one of the paradoxes of freedom and faith) be worked up by self-determined effort. Christ is the agent of the creation-affirming, person-saving act. He restores us to the condition of our creation so that our wills are able to respond to God's love. The world hospital has its own programs for acquiring this sense of rightness: by imitating heroes, by listening to wise teachers, by engaging in programs of self-improvement, by practicing a system of morality or ritual. Improvements are often experienced through these programs, but justification never takes place, for none of them deals with the primary person in the relationship, namely, God. God is the one with whom we must live if we will live freely to the outer limits of our humanity.

Not by Works of the Law

The second phrase is "not by works of the law." When we believe in justification by faith in Christ, we are freed from believing in many other things. The Christian is not a person who believes everything religious or moral or serious, but a person who makes a choice for a right relationship with God and against self-arranged improvement. In some ways Christians are the least religious people in town—there is so much that we don't believe! We don't believe in good-luck charms, in horoscopes, in fate. We don't believe the world's promises or the world's curses. And we don't believe—this comes to some as a surprise!—in good works.

Paul repeats the phrase "not by works of the law" three times in two verses. He means something quite specific by it. He means the acts that we perform in order to get God's approval. He means religious or moral activity that is designed to save our own skin. It is good behavior or religious behavior that is performed because someone else is looking, or because God is looking. It is life by performance, by show, by achievement. And, of course, it imprisons us because someone is always looking. We never have the pleasure of doing something just for the pleasure that it brings to someone or for the sense of rightness it has in our own lives. We must always be calculating what someone else will think of what we do, whether it will fit into what others expect, how God might reward us, what penalties we will avoid. We are back in the world hospital, keeping all the rules so that we will stay out of trouble and be approved by the people in charge. There is no free space in such a life to be oneself, to develop personal relationships, to accept and be accepted just as we are, speaking our mind, doing what is in our heart, adoring, believing, loving.

Found to Be Sinners

The third phrase is "found to be sinners." Reading between the lines of what Paul has written here, we might suspect that some gossipy persons have rummaged through Paul's life and discovered evidence that he was still—and maybe quite conspicuously—a sinner. And then, as if the test of a ministry of free grace versus a ministry of assigned works consisted in rating the highest moral performance, they noisily publicized what they found in order to repudiate his ministry. Paul's response is refreshing—and freeing.

"Why, of course, what did you expect? Aren't we all sinners?" The gossips had gone so far as to speculate that since Paul was a sinner and Christ was his partner, therefore Christ was an accessory to his sin!

Paul doesn't make excuses, doesn't deny, and he doesn't rationalize. He accepts the designation sinner without a trace of embarrassment. He is matter of fact about it. All of us are sinners. And we are not going to cease being sinners by redoubling our efforts at being good.

Living in the open means that we don't have to hide who we really are, whitewash our reputations or disguise our hearts. We can be open about who we are, about what we have thought and felt and done. We don't have to exhaust ourselves to project the blame for who we are on God or on our parents or on society. We don't have to make up fancy excuses.

How refreshing that is! People who are always blaming others for the difficulties they experience in life, who see their plight always as someone else's fault, who never see how they can do anything about the problems they have, are incapacitated for living freely. All their energy is directed toward convincing themselves and others that they are victims, and, of course, a victim is by definition hapless. But accepting ourselves just as we are puts us in touch with who we really are and discovers large tracts of responsibility in which we can experience forgiveness and out of which energies for creative new growth can flow in relationship with God.

Crucified with Christ

The fourth phrase is "crucified with Christ." The phrase is arresting and bold. The boldness intimidates some. The transition from hospital to world is too sudden. The timid retreat to the hospital where life is admittedly cramped, but at least there they know where they stand. There are

labels on things and people. There are lists that tell them
what to do. There are established procedures. Without
these labels and lists they feel unprepared for all the un-
knowns in the life of faith. They feel that they are not ready
to live the great truths. They admire Jesus from afar and
daydream about a different kind of life. They venture a
few steps into the open air and then, overcome with a sense
of timidity, shuffle back to their assigned spot in the closed
world of the hospital.

Paul, in contrast, plunges into life. There is no cautious
preparation; there is no long apprenticeship, no gradual
approaches, no preliminary meditation on the lilies of
the field. He embraces the dramatic climax: I was crucified
with Christ—cocrucified (*synestaurōmai*). Crucifixion ends
one way of life and opens up another. It finishes a life in
which the self is coddled and indulged and admired, and
begins a life that is offered to God and raised as a living
sacrifice.

The life of faith is not a matter of an occasional week-
end pass from the world's hospital, a few hours in which
we are given leave to see if we can manage it on our own
with God. It is not a matter, either, of a few select souls
who have been certified by the authorities to do all the
exciting things, while the lumpish middle class takes care
of filling the roles that society assigns them and a few hopeless cases learn to be meek by being sent on errands.

"The end is where we start from."[2] Everything that
Christ experienced we coexperience. Starting with Christ,
the complete revelation of Christ in crucifixion and resurrection, we live extravagantly, boldly and freely.

The Grace of God
The fifth phrase is "the grace of God." It is the atmosphere
in which everything else exists. In exploring the dimensions
of grace we approach existence not as those who take but

as those who receive. We do not rush into the world in order to plunder it. "I do not nullify the grace of God, for if justification were through the law, then Christ died to no purpose."

Grace means gift. Each morning we wake to a world and walk out of our houses to an existence that is given by God. God *shares* who he is and what he makes, his love and his salvation. He is not just maker of heaven and earth; he is not just the revealer of truth; he is not just architect of salvation. He gives. "For God so loved the world that he *gave...*"

If we will live freely, we will live receptively and gratefully. Personal explorations of grace develop freedom in relation to all persons and things. Where all is gift, I do not own things or persons and thus don't have to protect them. Therefore I don't have to be anxious. In a world of grace I do not live in laborious struggle trying to fashion a world that suits my needs and desires, hammering together a life out of the bits and pieces of scrap lumber that come my way. I do not live in anxious suspicion, nervous about what others might do to me, what others might think of me. I simply discover and receive.

All the great stories of exploration and discovery are parables of Christian venture. Columbus didn't sail across the ocean, decide to create a new continent, go back to Spain and organize a flotilla of ships to bring loads of dirt in order to make the Americas. It was already there. He discovered it and explored it. There is a world to enjoy, a salvation in which to rejoice. God gives. "Grace is everywhere."[3] We receive and explore. We do not nullify the grace of God.

Open Air

These five elements are characteristic of the atmosphere that is breathed in the free life in Christ. It is not pure air:

there is pollution—lies and insincerities and cynicism and
doubt. But at least it is open air. What must be rejected
out of hand is any return to the stifling existence of the
hospital of the world which only makes sense out of life
in terms of its sickness and sin.

That is what Peter was doing when Paul accosted him.
Peter was beating a retreat to the Hospital of the Holy Circumcision, but Paul prevented him: "Peter, don't do that—
that is the very place from which we have been released
—don't, by any means, go back. We are called and privileged to be pioneers in exploring the free country. We
are not sentenced to that high-security madhouse."

O foolish Galatians! Who has bewitched you, before whose eyes Jesus Christ was publically portrayed as crucified? Let me ask you only this: Did you receive the Spirit by works of the law, or by hearing with faith? Are you so foolish? Having begun with the Spirit, are you now ending with the flesh? Did you experience so many things in vain?—if it really is in vain. Does he who supplies the Spirit to you and works miracles among you do so by works of the law, or by hearing with faith?

Thus Abraham "believed God, and it was reckoned to him as righteousness." So you see that it is men of faith who are the sons of Abraham. And the scripture, foreseeing that God would justify the Gentiles by faith, preached the gospel beforehand to Abraham, saying, "In you shall all the nations be blessed." So then, those who are men of faith are blessed with Abraham who had faith.

For all who rely on works of the law are under a curse; for it is written, "Cursed be every one who does not abide by all things written in the book of the law, and do them." Now it is evident that no man is justified before God by the law; for "He who through faith is righteous shall live"; but the law does not rest on faith, for "He who does them shall live by them." Christ redeemed us from the curse of the law, having become a curse for us—for it is written, "Cursed be every one who hangs on a tree"—that in Christ Jesus the blessing of Abraham might come upon the Gentiles, that we might receive the promise of the Spirit through faith.

Galatians 3:1-14

7   Free to Think

CIRCUMCISION IS ONE OF THE most brilliantly conceived symbols of life in relationship to God. Semitic in origin, it has served that race for millennia as a symbol of a life intimate with God. Other religious rites combined with certain moral disciplines are also present, but over the centuries circumcision has acquired a singular prominence.

The symbolism of circumcision is both complex and obvious. There are layers on layers of meaning, but they are all accessible to the ordinary, reflective mind.

Circumcision is indisputably physical. Our relationship with God is not ethereal. It is not something that has to do with fine, mystical feelings. It is physical, earthy.

Circumcision is an operation on the most intimate member of the male body. It is not a decoration, like a tattoo. It is performed at the place which shows our essential identity, where we know and are known. Relationship with

God is not embroidery; it constitutes our character.

Circumcision is a wound. The scar remembers the pain of being separated from one way of life and set apart for another. We are not born innocent and pristine and then gradually fall away into sin; our natural condition requires intervention and is marked by an encounter with the divine, the holy.

Circumcision is vicarious. Each person does not have to bear the symbol in order to be in relationship with God. Since the sign was only carried by males, it could not be regarded as necessary for females who were obviously God's people quite as much as males. In that way the sign could never be identified with the reality itself. It was both necessary and not necessary.

The circumcised person is not whole but partial. The missing part is cut off by God's command, which command also supplies what is lacking. The visible sign of obedience to the command is also a sign of the invisible God who promises to redeem, to guide and to bless. God *cuts* his word into our lives, a covenant in which he commits himself to be our God. The circumcised person is a commanded person, an obedient person and a blessed person. Circumcision is a visible absence of flesh symbolizing the invisible presence of the Spirit, a sign of a life set free to be in right relation with God.[1]

It is understandable that such a symbol, carrying with it two thousand years of accumulated authority, would have the power to dazzle and impress, even to the extent of obscuring the reality it symbolized. And that is, in fact, what was happening in Galatia. They were identifying a symbolic appearance with a real presence. But appearance and reality are seldom the same. The earth appears to be flat; through a process of observation combined with reasoning, we conclude that it is round. The sun appears to revolve around the earth; through a process of observation combined with reasoning, we conclude that the earth moves around the sun. In the simpler areas of our lives direct observation and instinctual response unaided put us in touch with reality; but there are many areas, especially in areas of developed complexity, where rigorous reasoning is required to understand the relationship of appearance to reality. Life is complex. It increases in complexity from vegetable to animal to human. The highest form of life that we know is the free life. The appearances of such a life do not always correspond to the deepest realities. There are many movements and actions that appear to be free but which are only imitations of the current insanity. The ability to reason in relation to what is in our lives, to assemble all the evidence, visible and invisible, so that we can compare what is happening now with what happened last year, to hold what we experience with our senses in relation to what we receive by promise, to read Scripture accurately and our own hearts honestly is essential to living freely. It is the mind's task to do this complex work of holding these disparate and contrasting elements of appearance and reality together and to discern the created and redeemed order in and beneath them.

Persons who fail to think—that is, who fail to make rational connections between the visible and invisible, between what is right before our noses and what is sifted through the memories of generations—are bound to miss the point of many things and get mired in dead-end responses. Certain persons in the Galatian churches were missing the point of circumcision. They have always reminded me of my dog. When I point my finger and say to my dog "Look!" my dog sniffs my finger. For my dog, the pointing finger is not a sign, but simply a finger with texture and odor and taste. Likewise, there were some in the first century who, when the Hebrew traditions said "circumcision," could not recognize the rite as a sign pointing

to a reality, but simply looked at it and wouldn't quit looking at it. For as long as they were looking at the appearance,
they were not free to respond to the reality of a free life
with God.

Thinking, for the Christian, has never been either primary or final, neither the first matter nor the last. The life
of faith includes far more than can be comprehended or
analyzed by mere mind. But, all the same, the mind is a
marvelous gift and has important and essential functions in
the life of faith. There are times when it is the only means
given to us for discriminating between truth and error,
between sense and nonsense, between what is actual and
what is illusion, between the popular insanity of the age
and the enduring sanity of the gospel.

Paul, determined to do everything he can to develop a
sense of sanity in his congregations, detects elements of
craziness in his Galatian friends. There is nothing worse
than religion in which appearances are out of touch with
reality. Twice he calls attention to their foolishness in following this false teaching. Paul demands that they *think*
about their position and, in particular, their response to the
sign of circumcision. Paul shows himself here to be a relent-
less interrogator, putting five searching questions to them.
His questions are x rays that get past the appearances of
religion and put us in touch with the inner reality. Our
minds, unused, become captive to appearances. We need
frequent stimuli to shake loose from our dull, unthinking
state, to discern development and trace out relationships,
in short, to exercise our freedom to think.

*You crazy Galatians! Did someone give you a hallucinatory
drug? Something crazy has happened, for it is obvious that you no
longer have the crucified Christ in clear focus in your lives. He was
certainly set before you clearly enough. Let me put this question
to you: How did your new life begin? Was it by working your heads
off to please God? Or was it by responding to God's pleasure work-*

*ing in you? Are you going to continue this craziness? For only crazy
people would think they could complete by their own efforts what
was begun by God. If you weren't smart enough or strong enough
to begin it, how in heaven's name do you suppose you could perfect
it? Did you go through this whole painful learning process for
nothing? It is not yet for nothing, but it certainly will be if you keep
this up! Answer this question: Does the God who lavishly provides
you with his own presence, working things in your lives you could
never do for yourselves, does he do these things because of your
strenuous moral striving or because you let him do them in you?
Don't these things happen among you just as they happened with
Abraham who believed God, and that act of belief was turned into
a life of righteousness?*

*Is it not obvious to you that it is persons who believe (not persons
who are circumcised!) who are like Abraham? It was all laid out
beforehand in Scripture that God would justify the Gentiles by
faith. Scripture anticipated this in the gospel promise to Abraham,
"All nations will be blessed in you." So those now who live by faith
are blessed along with Abraham who lived by faith—this is no new
doctrine! And that means that anyone who tries to live independent-
ly of God by his own effort is doomed to failure. Scripture backs
this up: "Utterly cursed is every person who fails to carry out
every detail written in the book of law." The evident impossibility
of carrying out such a moral program should make it plain that
no one can sustain a relationship with God that way. The person
who lives in right relationship with God does it by letting God
arrange it for him. Doing things for God is the opposite of letting
God do things for you. Rule keeping does not naturally evolve
into living by faith, but only perpetuates itself in more and more
rule keeping, a fact observed in the scripture, "He who does these
things (namely, rule keeping) continues to live by them." Christ
redeemed us from that self-defeating, cursed life by absorbing it
completely into himself. Do you remember the scripture that says,
"Cursed is everyone who hangs on a tree"? That is what happened when Christ was nailed to the cross: he became a curse and at*

*the same time dissolved the curse. And now, because of that, the air
is cleared and we can see that Abraham's blessing is present and
available for Gentiles too. We are all able to receive God's life in
and with us by believing, just the way Abraham received it.*

A Sense of Proportion

The first of Paul's five questions gets us in touch with a
sense of proportion: "Who has bewitched you, before
whose eyes Jesus Christ was publicly portrayed as crucified?"

The single, overwhelming fact of history is the crucifixion of Jesus Christ. There is no military battle, no geo-
graphical exploration, no scientific discovery, no literary
creation, no artistic achievement, no moral heroism that
compares with it. It is unique, massive, monumental, unprecedented and unparalleled. The cross of Christ is not a
small secret that may or may not get out. The cross of Christ
is not a minor incident in the political history of the first
century that is a nice illustration of courage. It is the center.

An accurate perception of reality is marked by a sense of
proportion. A sane person is able to sort out what is more
important from what is less important and live appropriately. We learn to overlook some things as insignificant and
to take other things seriously. The inability to distinguish
proportions incapacitates us for living well.

For instance, all life is important and God-given, and
thus worth preserving. But not all of it has the same propor-
tionate value. When I am living sanely, I make distinctions.
If a tree in my front yard is diseased, I will try to restore it to
health in order to preserve its beauty and usefulness. And if
my child is ill, I will do what I can to preserve his life. But
with my child I will use all the money I have and all the
energy I have. I will not do that with the life of my tree.
Both lives are important, but a mind that is in touch with
reality is able to distinguish. There is a sense of proportion.

To use another example, dirt and mess are an offense to most of us, and so we clean them up. But healthy minds take into account proportions. If I entered the sanctuary where I lead worship each Sunday morning and found it littered with beer cans and strewn with spilled drinks and discarded food, I would go to the telephone in a panic and call a dozen or so parishioners to come to help me clean the place up before worship. But when I enter and notice an overlooked patch of dust on one of the pews or a cobweb in a corner, I do nothing. The dirt is there in both cases, but my congregation would judge me daft if I launched a religious crusade against dust devils and smudges. The pile of garbage and the speck of dust are both real, but the ability to discern their relative significance and to respond appropriately is a mark of sanity.

The cross of Christ is the central fact to which all other facts are subordinate. After his resurrection it became a symbol, not unrelated to circumcision, but far surpassing the earlier symbol in power and significance. But the Galatians were treating the cross as an item of religious trivia and circumcision as a crisis issue. What God did in showing his love for us and solving the problem of our sin is the central, foundational reality. It is not incidental but essential; it is not preliminary but conclusive. It is not background music but the center-stage drama. The cross placards that truth so that we are always aware that what God does for us is at the center of our lives.

Experience

A second question puts us in touch with our own experience. "Did you receive the Spirit by works of the law, or by hearing with faith?"

Spirit is the scriptural word for God sharing his life in our lives. It means that God is not an anonymous somebody "out there" or an idea explained in a book, but a living

presence whom I experience in the life I live day by day.
God gives himself to me. I receive God into myself. Spirit
is God's gift of himself in my experience.

People who are sane are in touch with their own experience. They assimilate and reflect on it, then make it their
own. People who are insane lose touch with their own experience. They become separated from their childhood,
no longer remembering or feeling the experiences of those
times. They become separated from what they did last
week, not able to integrate the experiences of certain emotional states like anger, or guilt, or shame, or joy into their
ongoing present.

Sanity means that we remember, conserve and use our
own experience. We are in touch with what has happened
to and in us. How did I become a person? Was it by doing
something significant so that one day my parents said,
"Wonderful, you just spoke a complete sentence; you are
now our son"? Or how did I first experience my own intelligence? When a teacher said, "You passed that examination with flying colors; that proves you have a mind"? Or
how did I experience the fact that I am a body? When a
physician said, "You came through that surgery beautifully; I opened you up and can verify that you have blood
and muscle and bone—you are a genuine body"? Or how
did I experience being a Christian? When a pastor exam-
ined the record of my performance and in a very pious
voice said, "Yes, I think that you qualify for God's love; here
is a certificate that will admit you to heaven"?

We are out of touch with reality when we need someone
else or some thing—circumcision? a baptismal certificate?
a bumper sticker? a pectoral cross?—to verify our existence. The sane person is in touch with relationships and
feelings and thoughts, and accepts that experience as primary. The primary experience is faith, the basic trust that
God is for us and shares his life with us. This basic trust

works itself through all our relationships and perceptions. If we forget that, we lose touch with what is basic to reality, become fragmented and at the mercy of isolated feelings or incidents or memories that never get lived coherently. The gospel keeps us in touch with our personal experience by bringing us back to the act of faith.

Common Sense
A third question puts us in touch with common sense. "Are you so foolish? Having begun with the Spirit, are you now ending with the flesh?"

Common sense is an aspect of sanity. Common sense is the ability to use our minds in relation to everyday reality. High intelligence, a well-trained mind and a large store of knowledge do not insure sanity. There are brilliant minds that are deranged. The test of sanity is whether we can make everyday, practical applications of our intelligence.

The gospel introduces us to a life that begins by receiving the life of God. God pours out his love for us. He mercifully provides access to forgiveness. All that is very exhilarating. It is a clear and vast improvement over living on the basis of appetites and impulses, getting and grabbing. We embark on the way of faith. We become free. We are filled with hope. We live more intensely and more amply than ever before.

Now, having begun there, what is the next step? What is the next step after love? Cautious mistrust? That is silly. What is the next step after faith? Anxious attempts to avoid anything that might displease God? That is silly. What is the next step after grace? Cannily bargaining with God so that we can manipulate him for our benefit? That is silly. That is like saying, "Having learned algebra, I will now go back to counting on my fingers."

"Use your heads," says Paul. Common sense ought to keep you from abandoning the gospel of grace. Only as we remain rooted in the gospel can we apply the great truths of love and forgiveness and grace to everyday affairs. When we hold firm to the gospel, what we experience in God we can continue to experience in our work and our play—when we read the newspaper and watch television, when we plan the spending of our money and when we respond to the demands and needs of family and friends.

Values
A fourth question puts us in touch with our values. "Did you experience so many things in vain?"

What is important to us? What is unimportant? A sane person has values. Some things are immensely important and cannot be discarded or ignored. Many persons never get their values clear and firm; they move by impulse. Some of them are in prison by reason of insanity.

What are our values? In the Christian way we acquire a healthy value system. We find that persons are more important than property. We learn that forgiveness is preferable to revenge. We realize that worshiping God is more central than impressing our neighbors.

When our values are denied or scorned by the people around us, will we abandon them? If we do, we will flounder. Without values we live "in vain." If we lose touch with our values, we are at the mercy of every seduction, every inducement, every claim on our money, our energy, our time. Values infuse life with a steady sense of direction and purpose. They free us from the petty dictatorships of fashion and fad and free us to pour ourselves into large goals for high purposes. The gospel keeps us in touch with sane and healthy values.

God
Paul's fifth question puts us in touch with God: "Does he who supplies the Spirit to you and works miracles among

you do so by works of the law, or by hearing with faith?"

This is similar to question two, but there is a different emphasis here. The more reality we are in touch with, the more sane we are. The gospel puts us in touch with the reality of God who richly gives, "who supplies the Spirit to you and works miracles among you." The important word is *supplies*. The Greek word for *supplies* *(epichoregeō)* is filled, etymologically, with gaiety. The root is "dance" *(choros)*. The noun is joined to the verb "lead" *(hegeomai)* to mean "lead a dance." In the course of usage that came to mean "to defray the cost of a dance," and then, metaphorically, "to furnish abundantly"—throw a lavish, celebrative dance. The word is further intensified with a prefixed preposition *(epi)*.[2] "Supply" is far too tame a translation. There is plenitude in God. That great fact must never be lost or obscured. We must not exchange this immense graciousness for a few scraps of human morality or a few shopworn proverbs. God is a vast reservoir of blessing who supplies us abundantly. If we lose touch with the reality of God, we will live clumsily and badly.

A wrong idea of reality leads to a wrong response to life. If we think God is stern and angry and despotic, we will live frightened. If we think that God is miserly and stingy, we will live feeling gypped. If we think that God is abstract and impersonal, we will live aimlessly and trivially. And how many people live that way—feeling scared, deprived, ignored and insignificant?

The gospel teaches us that in every way God supplies— he overflows with blessing and salvation. In touch with that reality we live with a sense of abandonment and walk with a confident gaiety, freely trusting, freely hoping, freely loving. Paul wants us to stay in touch with that reality.

The Sanity of the Gospel
A friend recently told me of a report given by a physician

specializing in the study of epidemics. The most severe disease in the world today is mental illness, and it is spreading. It is a worldwide epidemic. People all over the globe are less and less able to stay in touch with reality. People are going crazy at an alarming rate.

One of the reasons for this is that people live in a world of appearances that has no connection with reality. Their minds are no longer available for *thinking,* making connections between the visible and the invisible, aware of proportions, in touch with experience, active in common sense, committed to values, receptive to God's plenitude. The claim of the gospel is that it puts us in touch with reality— all of it, not just a part. It puts us in touch with a God who creates and with the people and world he created. It puts us in touch with a Christ who redeems and the people whom he loves. It puts us in touch with our feelings of hope and despair, with our thoughts of doubt and faith, with our acts of virtue and vice. It puts us in touch with everything, visible and invisible, right and wrong, good and evil. It puts us in touch and then trains us in mature ways of living.

We live in a world where people are going crazy. We have a gospel that sets us free to think, and in so doing it develops us in a rich and robust sanity. The sanity of the gospel is one of its most attractive features. Persons who truly live by faith are in touch with reality and become conspicuously sane.

To give a human example, brethren, no one annuls even a man's will, or adds to it, once it has been ratified. Now the promises were made to Abraham and to his offspring. It does not say, "And to offsprings," referring to many; but, referring to one, "And to your offspring," which is Christ. This is what I mean: the law, which came four hundred and thirty years afterward, does not annul a covenant previously ratified by God, so as to make the promise void. For if the inheritance is by the law, it is no longer by promise; but God gave it to Abraham by a promise.

Why then the law? It was added because of transgressions, till the offspring should come to whom the promise had been made; and it was ordained by angels through an intermediary. Now an intermediary implies more than one; but God is one.

Is the law then against the promises of God? Certainly not; for if a law had been given which could make alive, then righteousness would indeed be by the law. But the scripture consigned all things to sin, that what was promised to faith in Jesus Christ might be given to those who believe.

Now before faith came, we were confined under the law, kept under restraint until faith should be revealed. So that the law was our custodian until Christ came, that we might be justified by faith. But now that faith has come, we are no longer under a custodian; for in Christ Jesus you are all sons of God, through faith. For as many of you as were baptized into Christ have put on Christ.

Galatians 3:15-27

8   Free to Fail

AMONG THE APOSTLES, THE one absolutely stunning success was Judas, and the one thoroughly groveling failure was Peter. Judas was a success in the ways that most impress us: he was successful both financially and politically. He cleverly arranged to control the money of the apostolic band; he skillfully manipulated the political forces of the day to accomplish his goal. And Peter was a failure in ways that we most dread: he was impotent in a crisis and socially inept. At the arrest of Jesus he collapsed, a hapless, blustering coward; in the most critical situations of his life with Jesus, the confession on the road to Caesarea Philippi and the vision on the Mount of Transfiguration, he said the most embarrassingly inappropriate things. He was not the companion we would want with us in time of danger, and he was not the kind of person we would feel comfortable with at a social occasion.

Time, of course, has reversed our judgments on the two
men. Judas is now a byword for betrayal, and Peter is one
of the most honored names in church and world. Judas is a
villain; Peter is a saint. Yet the world continues to chase
after the successes of Judas, financial wealth and political
power, and to defend itself against the failures of Peter,
impotence and ineptness. But anyone who has learned the
first thing about freedom prefers to fail with Peter than to
succeed with Judas.

Any society that stresses success is bound to encourage
a maximum of security and a minimum of risk, and therefore to discourage freedom. "There is nothing so weak, for
working purposes," wrote Chesterton, "as this enormous
importance attached to immediate victory. There is nothing that fails like success."[1] It fails because it leaves out the
deeper dimensions of the human. Persons do not fail when
they are so thoroughly protected and guided that there is
always an intervening hand to prevent accident and to insure success. Persons do not fail when they live cautiously
and timidly, making sure that each task is well within their
capabilities, so that there is no risk of failure.

Monetary resources and political power are the usual
means of success. But the one is impersonal and the other
abstract; insofar as they encroach on the human they eliminate the capacity for freedom. For freedom is the unique
gift that is given to the human. Anything that tends toward
the impersonal (money) and the abstract (power) diminishes the capacity for freedom. Since success, as success is
counted in the world, relies heavily on money and power,
freedom is diminished. Judas's suicide is a parody of freedom.

And the failures? Are they the most free? Not necessarily. But those who are free to fail are the most free. Fear of
failure inhibits freedom; the freedom to fail encourages it.
The life of faith encourages the risk taking that frequently

results in failure, for it encourages human ventures into crisis and the unknown. When we are in situations where we are untested (like Peter at the arrest of Jesus) or unaccustomed (like Peter on the Mount of Transfiguration), we are sometimes going to fail, sometimes ignominiously. These failures, though, are never disasters because they become the means by which we realize new depths of our humanity and new vistas of divine grace. In the midst of our humanity and divine grace, the free life is shaped. "He who has never failed somewhere, that man cannot be great. Failure is the true test of greatness."[2]

Paul captures this insight and puts it to use in relation to the law. The law had been treated by many in his day as a means for achieving a secure, successful life. Paul turned that position on its head and showed that the law, in fact, made it impossible for anyone to be a success, exposing everyone instead as a failure. When the law is taken seriously and used according to its intent, it exposes us all, mercilessly and relentlessly, as failures. The law, as Paul came to understand it, assumed that we would fail and did nothing to prevent it. It left us free to fail. In Paul's exposition, failure is not a thing to be avoided, but an inevitability to be faced and lived through. The law is God's direction for facing failure and living it through.

Friends, let me give you an example from everyday affairs of the free life I am talking about. Once a person's will has been ratified, no one annuls it or adds to it. Now, the gospel promises were made to Abraham and to his offspring. You will note that Scripture, in the careful language of a legal document, does not say "to offsprings," referring to everybody in general, but "to your offspring" (the noun, note, is singular) referring to Christ. This is the way I interpret this: A will, earlier ratified by God, is not annulled by a codicil that is attached 430 years later, negating the promise of the will. This codicil, with its instructions and regulations, has nothing to do with the promise in the will.

What is the point, then, of the law, the attached codicil? It was a thoughtful addition to guide sinful and restless people until Christ (the offspring) came, inheriting the promises and distributing them to us. Obviously this law was not firsthand encounter with God; it was arranged by angelic messengers through the hand of the mediator Moses. But if there is a mediator, as there was at Sinai, we are not dealing directly with God, are we? But the basic promise is the unmediated blessing of God, received by faith.

If such is the case, is the law then an antipromise, a negation of God's will for us? Not at all. Its purpose was to make obvious to everyone that we are, in ourselves, out of right relationship with God, and therefore to show us the futility of devising some religious system for getting on our own efforts what we can only get by waiting in faith for God to complete his promise. For if any kind of rule keeping had power to create life in us, we would certainly have gotten it by this time.

Until the time when we were mature enough to respond freely in faith to the living God, we were carefully surrounded and protected by the Mosaic law. The law was like those Greek pedagogues, with which you are familiar, who escort children to school and protect them from danger or distraction, making sure the children really will get to the place they set out for. But now you have arrived at your destination: by faith in Christ you are in direct relationship with God. Your baptism in Christ was not just washing you up for a fresh start, it also involved dressing you in an adult faith wardrobe, Christ's life, the fulfillment of God's original promise.

Footnote to Faith

The free life begins with Abraham—and Abraham's life was a faith life. Moses must always be subordinate to Abraham. The law must always be a footnote to faith. But in Paul's earlier experience Moses had become the textbook for the successful life and Abraham served as a mere preface. By this radical shift of proportions, the very nature of Moses' law was turned inside out: instead of its being used to keep failures in the life of faith from ending in despair, instead of its being used to guide untested human beings in their faith pilgrimage, the law was used as a handbook for success—a set of rules which, if followed, would eliminate risk, venture and growth from life, and insure a perfect performance approved by God and admired by society. Paul now restores the original proportions: Abraham, a thorough and complete exposition of the free life of faith; Moses, an important but minor supplement to encourage and guide us through the failures that are normal in the life of faith.

At the church which I serve as pastor there are arrows painted on the access lanes to the parking lot. One lane has a prominent arrow indicating that it is an entrance; the other, an arrow that indicates that it is an exit. The arrows are placed there to direct traffic in and out of our parking lot so that we don't bang each other's fenders. Most people follow the arrows.

But some don't. One person whom I know well consistently defies the arrows. I asked her about it one day. She admitted that it wasn't mere carelessness but something quite deliberate. Not, to be sure, a major rebellion against law and order, but a minor act of defiance. No one, she said, by painting a white mark on the asphalt was going to decide which of two lanes she would use to get to the place where she would worship God. Besides, she admitted, it made her feel good to assert her personal free will against that impersonal regulation.

I had been following the arrows, unthinkingly, for years. If the arrow said do it, I did it. How should I respond to my friend? One possibility I considered was, "Listen, if you want to come to this church, you play by our rules. We want to get people into this church as safely and conveniently as possible; we have provided those arrows so that will happen; I will explain to you why they are necessary, and then

I will expect you to keep the rules. If you ignore them, you are no longer welcome."

In my imagination I anticipated her reply, "Hey, you are making a big deal out of nothing. The important thing is that I get to church, isn't it? Worshiping God, loving my neighbor, encouraging my friends, accepting the gift of grace—they are what matters!" And I would then say, "Yes, but you have to do it in certain orderly ways. We have carefully worked things out. If you don't follow the arrows, somebody is going to get killed and then you will be sorry, or some visitor is going to get his fender crumpled and never come back to church again."

That kind of discussion has been taking place in and around churches for twenty centuries. We are Christians, set free for access to God. As we enjoy and exercise that freedom, the experience is supplemented by wisdom expressed in rules that provide useful guidance. A later generation omits the experience, keeps the rules and makes a religion out of them. One day some people caught Paul going against the arrows; a committee confronted him on the church parking lot in Galatia and challenged him. They were formidable and irate. At the time it might have seemed easier to agree and go along with the committee. But Paul discerned a larger issue and took a stand. He wasn't going to let anyone or anything supplant the freedom of faith.

Arrows for Freedom
The question keeps coming up, Then what are the arrows for? Are you going to make every one follow the arrows? And if you decide that you aren't—since the arrows are not original or necessary—why not just get rid of them altogether?

What place does the law have in the life of faith? It certainly has a place. Some say too much of a place; others say not enough of a place. Nobody has handled the question better than Paul. His understanding and response to the question of what to do about the arrows (the law) has preserved the sanity and health and freedom of Christians. The root meaning of *law (torāh)* in Hebrew is "to throw something." But it is not a random throw; it is a directed throw, like an arrow that will hit its mark.[3] It is, thus, a "sense of divine direction."[4] As long as the law arrows are used that way, they support the free life of faith.

So Paul's first point is this: Before we can use the law skillfully and freely, we have to have something to use it on, which means that we have to be thoroughly involved in the life of faith. The first response of our lives to God is the act of faith. Until we abandon ourselves to that, nothing else will make sense.

Paul argues the primacy of faith by centering attention on Abraham. "The promises were made to Abraham" (3:16). Abraham is the towering figure of faith in our tradition. We know so little about the man, and yet he means so much to us. We know only a few bare details. Somewhere in the shadows of the nineteenth century B.C. in Ur of the Chaldees, in a corner of the Persian Gulf that is once more a center of world attention, he heard God's call, left home and began a long trek westward. He left his religion, his home, his culture and his security. God was more important to Abraham than anything else—country, comfort, culture. Abraham listened to God. Abraham obeyed God. Abraham believed God.

From those few stories, and some spare comments on them, we come to discover a radically new way of life, a life of faith. God offers himself in personal relationship with us; we respond with nothing less than our lives. Everything in and about us—our work, our families, our affections, our plans, our memories, our play, our possessions—is coordinated and arranged in that foundational, responding, living relationship with God. I live by what God says, not by what I can discover; I move in accordance with God's promise, not by my ambition; I venture boldly into a life where I am directed, instead of cowering in an imprisoning security in which I am afraid to make a move lest I offend God or a neighbor.

Life opens up. Instead of the stuffy, ponderous life of Ur in the Chaldees—rich, oppressive, monotonous—there is a wind-blown life in the austere desert, a place that is empty of human achievement but full of opportunity to respond to the great invisibles of grace and love and hope. Life becomes adventure, growth, exploration, faith.

Abraham was the person for whom the invisible was more real than the visible. What God said to him was more important than what man said about him. He chose to live extravagantly and recklessly by promise rather than cautiously on a guaranteed income from the Chaldean banks. He chose to live the free life.

No AAA Map

And where is there any talk of law in all of that? Can you find any arrows painted in that wilderness into which Abraham ventured? Did he have a rule book that showed him step by step what he must do to please God? Did he have an AAA map which showed all the best hotels and oasis rest stops between Ur and Canaan? No, he lived by faith. He was living in response to God, obeying God, consulting God, being changed by God, being challenged by God, growing in relationship to God, listening to God, praising God, believing God.

Did Abraham have a twenty-year plan with carefully defined objectives as he launched his important career as father of the faithful? No, there were delays, interruptions, detours, failures. He didn't do it all correctly—he didn't live without doubt or sin or despair—but he did it. He followed and confessed and prayed and believed. God was alive for him. God was the center for him.

We don't live by faith by reading a rule book, or following a map, or working through a career development program, or following the arrows.[5] We do not begin with things, or pieces of paper, or ideas, or feelings, or deeds, or successes. Especially not successes, because we have learned that every success is an abstraction which turns a person into an empty shell. Any formula that prevents failure also prevents freedom.[6] We begin with God. We dare to believe that God cares who we are, knows who we are. We dare to believe that God is the reality beyond and beneath and around all things, visible and invisible, and that he provides for us and loves and blesses and saves us.

"Don't you realize," said Paul to the people who were trying to get him to follow the success formula of the arrows, "that those arrows, the law, didn't even appear for 430 years after Abraham? For nearly five hundred years men and women lived by faith without benefit of law. They had nothing to tell them how to get from here to there, nothing to regulate their actions, nothing in black and white to explain or define God." (And in the church where I am pastor people worshiped for ten years before anybody thought to paint arrows on the driveways).

A Temporary Custodian
"Why then the law?" Is it useless? Is it a contradiction to faith that lives by God's promises? Maybe we should simply throw it out and let everyone do things on their own.

But those arrows are useful, aren't they? At its best, Judaism was full of enthusiasm for the law. Psalms 19 and 119 cannot find enough good to say about it. The law is always pointing to a relationship with God, always giving insight into the way we live in the presence of a God who blesses and redeems and creates right relationships. It

points us in the right direction, to the personal divine center of all of life. It conserves the insights of persons of faith
so that living by faith isn't blind trial and error, living by
guesswork and hazard. Paul is appreciative and full of
praise for this. The law has directional quality to it. It shows
us the way to God, the quickest, most economical way without getting snarled in a moral traffic jam. Von Hugel says
somewhere that we do not live our days with the aim of
pleasing the police, but we do "follow the police regulations, since, by so doing, we find that we can more fully and
easily live our day in a worthy manner."[7]

The law becomes an obstruction only when people stupidly reduce the act of coming to worship God to a small-
minded ritual of following the arrows, "keeping the law."
Imagine it: people slowly, cautiously driving their cars into
a church parking lot, following the arrows, careful not to
drive over any of the parking lines, and then driving out,
still following the arrows, and then back again, driving
around and around and around and never getting out of
the car to sing and pray and listen and give, or coming in to
worship a living God with a live and joyous congregation
of persons who are freely living the promises of God by
faith. That is what some people were doing in Paul's Galatian churches. It is what some people continue to do in
churches today.

But we aren't going to cure them by getting rid of the arrows, by discarding the law, but only by living by faith and
using the law. Paul provides a good illustration to show exactly how the law works, how the law can be understood and
used, and not just "kept." He calls the law a custodian: "The
law was our custodian until Christ came." The meaning of
the Greek word *paidagōgos* that lies behind the English word
custodian often loses something in translation. Greek families that were well enough off to have slaves chose one of
them, usually an old and trusted slave, to be in charge of

their child or children from the ages of six to sixteen. This custodian went with the child to school to see that no harm or mischief came to him. He was not the schoolmaster. He had nothing to do with the actual teaching of the child. It was only his duty to take him safely to the school and deliver him to the teacher. That, says Paul, is how the law works: it delivers us to the place of faith, to Christ.[8]

The law is just such a custodian, a slave assigned to a free person for a strictly functional purpose. The slave doesn't rule the free child. And the slave is quite temporary—only during the time when there is special need for protection and guidance. But have you ever heard of a free adult letting a slave lead him around to work, to play, to church? The law is a good slave, but a bad master.

But, having arrived at adulthood, are we free from failure and guaranteed a life of success? Of course not. We are legally free from parental supervision; we are mentally free to think whatever thoughts we wish; we are emotionally free to make attachments or to indulge resentments. Possibilities burgeon. "We are at our human finest," exults Lewis Thomas, "dancing with our minds, when there are more choices than two. Sometimes there are ten, even twenty different ways to go, all but one bound to be wrong, and the richness of selection in such situations can lift us onto totally new ground. This process is called exploration and is based on human fallibility."[9]

We venture and choose—and we fail. We are not free from failure. We find that the good intentions of our parents have not always worked out for our good. Strings have been attached to their feelings and thoughts that inhibit and restrict us. We find that our teachers were not always honest and that our minds therefore have distorted and inadequate ideas that keep us from getting a clear and accurate picture of reality. We find that we want to be good, to be whole, and that we are not. Try as we might, yearn as we will, we are not. We are unfinished. At the very time that parents and society, school and business certify us as free persons, we realize that we are not free for what we want most of all—to be complete. We are free to do many things. We are free from many restrictions. But what about the center? What about God?

There we live by faith and failure, by faith and forgiveness, by faith and mercy, by faith and freedom. We do not live successfully. Success imprisons. Success is an unbiblical burden stupidly assumed by prideful persons who reject the risks and perils of faith, preferring to *appear* right rather than to *be* human.

There is neither Jew nor Greek, there is neither slave nor free, there is neither male nor female; for you are all one in Christ Jesus. And if you are Christ's then you are Abraham's offspring, heirs according to promise.

I mean that the heir, as long as he is a child, is no better than a slave, though he is the owner of all the estate; but he is under guardians and trustees until the date set by the father. So with us; when we were children, we were slaves to the elemental spirits of the universe. But when the time had fully come, God sent forth his Son, born of woman, born under the law, to redeem those who were under the law, so that we might receive adoption as sons. And because you are sons, God has sent the Spirit of his Son into our hearts, crying, "Abba! Father!" So through God you are no longer a slave but a son, and if a son then an heir.

Formerly, when you did not know God, you were in bondage to beings that by nature are no gods; but now that you have come to know God, or rather to be known by God, how can you turn back again to the weak and beggarly elemental spirits, whose slaves you want to be once more? You observe days, and months, and seasons, and years! I am afraid I have labored over you in vain.

Galatians 3:28–4:11

9 Free to Receive

*R*ECEIVE IS A FREEDOM WORD. *Take* is not. To receive is to accept what the divine largess provides for us. To take is to plunder whatever is not nailed down. To receive is to do what children do in the family. To take is to do what pirates do on the high seas.

All studies of the loss of freedom are stories of *taking:* Adam and Eve taking the fruit from the tree, Prometheus taking fire from the gods, Siegfried taking the gold from the Nibelung. All the stories of access to freedom are stories of *receiving.* The most powerful of all these stories is that of the Christian Eucharist in which Christ's disciples receive the sacramental bread and wine. This story continues to be told, re-enacted and believed by persons who, set free, live freely.

The difference between receiving and taking is deeply interior. It has to do with a disposition of spirit, an act of

faith, an openness to God. Outwardly similar, even identi-
cal, physical actions constitute both taking and receiving.
Verbally the words can be used in many contexts inter-
changeably. The Greek word *lambanō* is used for both
receiving and taking. But the similarities are all on the surface; by observing context and continuities we can easily
distinguish taking, with all its ambitious assertion and
prideful aggrandizement, from receiving, with all its grateful acceptance and humble receptivity. Rarely is there any
difficulty in deciding how to translate the word—moral
and spiritual dispositions are not easily concealed. But Paul
guards against even a hint of ambiguity in the passage at
hand by using a form of *lambanō* that can only mean receive
(*apolambanō*).

*In Christ's family there can be no division into Jews and Greeks,
slaves and free, male and female. Among us you are all equal; that
is, we all are in a common relationship to Jesus Christ. Also, since
you are Christ's family, then you are Abraham's famous "offspring," heirs according to the promises to Abraham and his offspring that I referred to before.*

*Let me show you the implications of this: as long as the heir is
a minor he has no advantage over the slave; though legally he owns
the entire inheritance, he is subject to tutors and administrators
until whatever date the father has set for emancipation. That is
the way it is with us: when we were minors we were just like slaves
ordered around by fate (the tutors and administrators of this world),
with no say in the conduct of our own lives. But when the date
arrived that was set by God the Father for us to receive our inheritance, God sent his Son, actually born among us of a woman, born
under the conditions of the law so that he might redeem us who
have been kidnaped by the law. Thus we have been set free to experience our rightful sonship. Because you are now children, God sent
the Spirit of his Son into our lives crying out, "Abba! Father!"
Doesn't that privilege of intimate conversation with God make it
plain that you are not a slave, but a child, and if a child, then*

an heir, with complete access to the inheritance?

Earlier, before you knew God personally, you were enslaved to so-called gods that had nothing of the divine about them. But now that you know God—or rather since God knows you—how can you possibly subject yourselves again to that sickly and beggarly old woman Fate and be bossed around by her? For that is what you do when you are intimidated into scrupulously observing all the taboos and superstitions associated with special days and seasons and years. I am afraid that all my hard work among you has gone up in a puff of smoke!

Slaves or Heirs?

Freedom is what we receive from God, who himself is free and who wills us to be free. It is not what we rebelliously demand as a right or defend in perpetual paranoia as a possession. It begins in a kind of trusting passivity, not in rebellious assertion. This approach to freedom is thoroughly alien to the literature and rhetoric of the modern and western world which places an inordinately high premium on taking: freedom is something outside ourselves that waits to be grabbed—through a course in assertiveness training, through breaking out of the bonds of marriage, through the violence of revolution. The premise behind this approach is that freedom is something that is *there,* which we must *take.* Paul's guidance is far different: freedom is something that is *here,* which we have only to *receive.* Paul uses, with great effectiveness, a metaphor to develop the interior dynamics of receiving freedom. His metaphor is of a father who has executed a will that decrees that his children live freely. The personal will of the father is made explicit in a legal will that names each child (each person!) as an heir.

Implicit in Paul's position here is that if we are ignorant of the real situation regarding ourselves and Christ, we will fail to live freely. If we are ignorant of ourselves—miscon-

ceive ourselves as slaves rather than as sons and daughters
—we will either feel powerless and live in apathy, or we will
fight every step of the way in a hopeless kind of fury that
knows the chances of liberation are slim. If we are ignorant
of Christ, even though we have a high regard of ourselves,
we will not know that the time of our emancipation has
come, and so we will live in reverie and fantasy, dreaming
of future conquests. Everything of significance will be de-
ferred to the future when we come of age. We will see ourselves perhaps as sons and daughters, but as minors nonetheless, incapable of responsible activity, inexperienced in
acts of risk, fearful of suffering and pain. We will live in a
narrow, albeit comfortable, world of secure convention.

The person who is a slave knows that freedom is outside
his or her status, outside of what is natural; freedom therefore must be seized. Unemancipated children know that
they must wait for freedom. Freedom lies in the future and
can only be enjoyed in acts of the dreaming imagination.
But in regard to God's will executed in Christ no one is a
slave, no one is an unemancipated child. We are sons and
daughters come of age, with access to the complete inheritance. Grabbing is out. Fantasizing is out. Receiving is the
mode of access to freedom.

Free in Relationship
The metaphor radiates insights. Son or daughter is a word
of relationship. Freedom is the experience of being a person in relationship to God. The word *son* or *daughter* does
not describe us biologically or economically or psychologically or historically, but personally. It means being ourselves not in isolation but in relation—with God. We are
not free if we are separated from significant reality. For
instance, we are not free if we are sent into exile in the
desert, even though we are free in that desert to do anything we like, because we are not free to be with the people

who are important to us. For that reason exile was one of the most feared punishments of the ancient world. Freedom has far more to do with relationships than with geography.

The more we consider it, the more we can see why son or daughter is just the right word to describe the experience of freedom. It emphasizes everything that makes us who we are. It takes our personhood with complete seriousness, but at the same time holds it all in relationship to the one who originated our life and who continues as the most important being in our lives, namely, God.

So what is it like to live free? It is like being a son or a daughter. As Paul ponders and lives out this experience of freedom he fills in details of what it is like day by day.

Equally Free
In living free we discover our essential equality with everyone else. "There is neither Jew nor Greek, there is neither slave nor free, there is neither male nor female; for you are all one in Christ Jesus." The experience of being a child in a family is an unfolding realization of a basic equality in worth and relationship.

We don't always experience this in our own families, but we understand that it is possible for a parent to love each child equally. All the children in a family are different—different sizes, different states of health, different temperaments, different degrees of goodness and badness, differences in intelligence. And the parent deals with each differently. But the same love and wisdom is exercised in relation to each. We at our best (and we not always are) do not have favorite children. God at his best (and he always is) does not have favorite children.

How freeing it is to discover that! Other people then are no longer a threat to our security or our chances of being recognized and loved. We are not rivals competing for a prize, but participants in a common life, brothers and sisters in a single family. We are free to accept, even glory in, our diversity.

The biblical story of creation makes it clear that the great variety in creation is not a matter of some things being better and other things being worse. The repeated refrain is "And God saw that it was good." The diversity is goodness abundantly expressed. In Paul's sermon to the Athenians he said, "And he made from one every nation of men to live on all the face of the earth" (Acts 17:26). We have a common origin; we have a common nature; we have a common destiny; we have a common Lord.

But we are not the same. "Nobody is really quite like anyone else; there are reminders here and there, but no exact duplicates; we are four billion unique individuals."[1] We don't all look alike, or feel alike, or act alike. But instead of freely celebrating our glorious diversities, we often allow sin to twist those differences into occasions for pride or humiliation or covetousness or envy, robbing us of our freedom. Racial and national differences become expedients for treating persons as commodities or as consumers. Sexual differences become ruses for exploitation and lust. In every case, the presence of the other person different from me encroaches on my freedom, narrows my life, constricts my living space, deprives me of my dignity. I am not free if I am treated as something less or other than human. I am not free if only part of me is recognized—my race, or my sex, or my possessions, or my reputation.

As a son or daughter in Christ all these differences of race (Greek and Jew), of status (slave and free), of sex (male and female) which provoke envy and make enemies are subordinated to the central, common relationship which we have in Christ. Now all those basic harmonies and continuities in which we are created can be experienced and developed. We are free in relationship to each other, discovering an equal acceptance. Other persons are not enemies to fear, not superior beings to envy, not deadbeats to avoid. In Christ every person is or can be experienced in a new way, a person we are free to receive and love without fear of being diminished or intimidated.

Priceless Treasures
When we live free we also begin to discover our immense worth. Sons and daughters are priceless to a parent. We cannot be compared to a possession or to a function. Our worth is staggering and incalculable when considered from a parent's view of a child's worth.

All of us grow up with an inferiority complex. Some of us are able to disguise it better than others, but the feelings of inferiority are there all the same. One reason is that during the most formative years of our lives, we were small, less knowledgeable, weaker and less experienced than the important people in our lives (parents, teachers, older children in the neighborhood). There was always someone around who was better than we were in some way or other. We lose some of those feelings as we mature, but never entirely. We are always vulnerable to self-doubt. Am I worth anything at all? Does anyone care if I really exist? If I disappeared tomorrow, how long would it take before everything was normal? A week, a month, a year? We try in various ways to become indispensable to people around us so that we can have our significance verified, but our efforts are not convincing.

We cannot experience freedom when we live that way. A feeling of inadequacy is enslaving. No matter how free we are told that we are, if we don't think we are worth anything, we will not be motivated to express our strengths, will not be confident in developing our gifts, will not feel up to enjoying the blessings of the day.

The gospel counters that enslaving experience by telling

the story of our redemption: "We were slaves to the elemental spirits of the universe. But when the time had fully come,
God sent forth his Son, born of woman, born under the law,
to redeem those who were under the law, so that we might
receive adoption as sons." That action-packed sentence is a
powerful description of Christ's great work on behalf of all
of us. One word in it tells us what we are worth: *redeem*.

All Paul's readers would have been familiar with the first-
century Greek process for freeing slaves. The word *redeem*
describes this process. Sometimes a slave caught the attention of a wealthy free person and for some reason or other
—compassion, affection, justice—the free person decided
to free the slave. The free person would then go to the temple or shrine and deposit with the priests the sum of money
required for manumission. The priests would then deliver
an oracle: The god Apollo has purchased this slave so-and-
so from owners such-and-such and is now free. The priests
then passed the redemption price on to the recent owner.
The exslave who all his or her life had been treated as an
inferior, useful only for purposes of running someone
else's errands, doing someone else's work, was no longer
subject to such evaluation. The person was free. No price
could be put on that head again. The person was valuable
not to *do* something but to *be* someone.

That, says Paul, is what has happened to each and everyone of us: we have been singled out for redemption. A price
has been paid to free us.[2] When I hear that story I realize
what worth I have. I am valuable beyond calculation. God
singled me out and paid the price to set me free from slavery. Now that I am a son I am treated with all the undivided
attention and special care that is inherent in such a relationship. There is no one quite like me. That doesn't mean that
I am better than any others, but it does mean that I am
unique. With such a sense of worth I experience freedom in
deeper and wider dimensions than ever before.

Family Intimacy
When we live free we also become aware of our intimacy
with God. Paul describes this intimacy in the use of the word
Abba: "Because you are sons, God has sent the Spirit of his
Son into our hearts, crying, 'Abba! Father!' "

Abba is an Aramaic word. Aramaic is the language of
first-century Palestine and the native speech of Jesus. Abba
means Father, but in a colloquial, intimate sense. The nearest equivalent in our language is Daddy, or perhaps Papa.

In Christ we are introduced into an unprecedented intimacy with God. Nowhere in the Old Testament do we find
God addressed as Father. He is sometimes described as a
father, but not addressed familiarly as Father—Papa,
Abba. But Jesus always addressed God in this way in his
prayers, the way children in everyday talk address their
fathers.[3] The gift of sonship confers the privilege of the
child to address the father with intimacy.

Suddenly we are free with God, like a child is free with
a parent. We are not involved in stiff, formal protocols in
relation to God. We don't have to be afraid lest we put our
foot in our mouth, or embarrass ourselves, or get sent out
of the room because we didn't use the right title. We can
address God as freely as we address our parents. It is the
kind of freedom that combines intimacy with reverence.
We are still aware of the majesty and awesome glory of God.
We do not try to reduce God to a level of coziness where
we can manipulate him. The intimacy is a freedom to share
ourselves, to express ourselves fearlessly in God's presence.
We are free to be spontaneous, personal and uninhibited.
Faith is not a formal relationship hedged in with elaborate
courtesies; it is a family relationship, intimate and free.

Freedom Now
The clause "when the time had fully come" insists that
all that has been given by God and received in personal

relationship be realized now. It is Paul's equivalent of Jesus' inaugural emphasis: "The time is fulfilled, and the kingdom of God is at hand; repent and believe in the gospel" (Mk 1:15). Everything that God has planned and prepared and executed is available now. "The highest densities of meaning lie in the immediate, in the most obviously 'at hand.' "[4]

The present moment more resembles eternity than any other, because in the present, the past and the future converge. The refusal or the inability to fully experience the present, to receive into our lives by faith what is handed to us by God in the present, is a refusal to live freely. For the present is the only time in which freedom can be exercised or experienced.

A preference for living in the past is nostalgia. There are many solaces and rewards that accompany nostalgia, and therefore many who indulge in it. But for all its comforts it is a dreamy dilution of our being. We lose relationship and intimacy; we lose responsibility; we lose ecstasy. And we lose freedom. The past is highly useful as the sifted experience of the race. It provides impetus and wisdom for intense living in the present. But as an excuse for reverie it is simply sin. The golden age for the Christian is never the past. We do not look back to the time of revolution when freedom was won in glorious battle and then try to recreate the best moments in mock battles and period uniforms. We do not reminisce about the good old days. Rather we immerse ourselves wholeheartedly in a present for which the past provides a solid foundation of promise.

A preference for living in the future is fantasy. It too has its solaces and rewards. But for all its attractions it also is a dreamy dilution of our essential being. We lose sensory intensities; we lose the stimulus of crisis; we lose the complex mysteries of mixed spirit and matter. The future is highly useful to us as an articulation of hope that gives us a sense of purpose, providing focus and direction. But the future as an escape into fantasy is a sin.

Paul's word *heir* set alongside the phrase "time fully come" gathers the three aspects of time into a free present. The word *heir* particularly describes the person whose promised past and anticipated future dovetail into a present moment of realized freedom. And the phrase "time fully come" emphasizes that this present is no mere present, but a complex present. Thomas Hardy describes his incurably superficial and frivolous Sergeant Troy as a "man to whom memories were an incumbrance, and anticipations a superfluity. Simple feeling, considering, and caring for what was before his eyes, he was vulnerable only in the present."[5] Paul, although as insistently in the present as Sergeant Troy, is in every other way a contrast and far freer. Freedom is not frivolity.

In the Apocalypse, St. John's original and arresting title for Jesus as the one "who is and who was and who is to come" (Rev 1:8) begins with the present, gathers up the past and draws in the future so that the present is no mere moment but the intense and immense "fullness of time" where freedom is received and lived.

It is in the present, and only in the present, that time is fulfilled, completed and consummated. The gospel kingdom is saturated with time in all aspects—present, past and future—but they converge on the present. "My future," wrote Ortega, "makes me discover my past in order to realize that future. The past is now real because I am re-living it, and it is when I find in the past the means of realizing my future that I discover my present. And all this happens in an instant; moment by moment life swells out into the three dimensions of the true interior time. The future tosses me back toward the past; the past toward the present, and from here I go again toward the future which throws me back to the past, and the past to another present, in a constant rotation."[6]

The heir living in fulfilled time is in a position to "recover the full meaning of freedom."[7] Slaves live within predictable limitations; sons and daughters live within expanding opportunities. We are free to receive. We do not have to live off the diminishing capital of a sum which was deposited to our account in the past, so that each day means that there is less to live on than the day before. We are not subject to diminishing opportunities, diminishing energies, diminishing freedom. Each day now opens out into a *more*.

Brethren, I beseech you, become as I am, for I also have become as you are. You did me no wrong; you know it was because of a bodily ailment that I preached the gospel to you at first; and though my condition was a trial to you, you did not scorn or despise me, but received me as an angel of God, as Christ Jesus. What has become of the satisfaction you felt? For I bear you witness that, if possible, you would have plucked out your eyes and given them to me. Have I then become your enemy by telling you the truth? They make much of you, but for no good purpose; they want to shut you out, that you may make much of them. For a good purpose it is always good to be made much of, and not only when I am present with you. My little children, with whom I am again in travail until Christ be formed in you! I could wish to be present with you now and to change my tone, for I am perplexed about you.

Tell me, you who desire to be under law, do you not hear the law? For it is written that Abraham had two sons, one by a slave and one by a free woman. But the son of the slave was born according to the flesh, the son of the free woman through promise. Now this is an allegory: these women are two covenants. One is from Mount Sinai, bearing children for slavery; she is Hagar. Now Hagar is Mount Sinai in Arabia; she corresponds to the present Jerusalem, for she is in slavery with her children. But the Jerusalem above is free, and she is our mother. For it is written, "Rejoice, O barren one who does not bear; break forth and shout, you who are not in travail; for the children of the desolate one are many more than the children of her that is married."

Now we, brethren, like Isaac, are children of promise. But as at that time he who was born according to the flesh persecuted him who was born according to the Spirit, so it is now. But what does the scripture say? "Cast out the slave and her son; for the son of the slave shall not inherit with the son of the free woman." So brethren, we are not children of the slave but of the free woman.

Galatians 4:12-31

10 Free to Trust

A MAN WALKED INTO AN automobile showroom. Several models of new cars were on display. The floor was carpeted. The lighting was exciting and stimulating. There were photographs of happy, pleased people sitting in and driving these splendid machines along ocean beaches and through cool forests. A smiling, affable person met the man and took an immediate interest in him. Names were exchanged. A woman appeared with a tray of coffee. The two men sat down on expensively crafted furniture. Within minutes they were conversing like old friends. The man felt important, attractive, valued.

Models of cars were discussed. Marvelous features, miracles of scientific technology, were held up for admiration. Then suddenly the man hesitated; he voiced some qualms. Maybe he ought to talk this over with a friend, maybe wait a couple of days before making a decision. The hesitation was skillfully parried by his new friend, and within moments the man knew beyond the shadow of a doubt that the urgent need of his life was getting one of those cars. And the man with him was going to help him get it. Difficulties were overcome. Obscure items were explained. The steps that had to be negotiated were outlined. Every minute with his new friend left him feeling more intelligent, more in control of his life, master of the mysteries of finance and technology.

In a couple of hours the man left the place more complete than he had felt for a long time, the owner of a new car. He had a sense of freedom and pleasure as the powerful engine and expertly engineered machine responded to his command. And he had this marvelous new friend who had helped him get it and promised to continue to help him in the future. It was far more than a crass, commercial transaction; there were dimensions of hospitality and intimacy that were beyond money. Getting that car wasn't just acquiring a means of transportation; the man himself became different somehow. He experienced a glow, a sense of well-being, an affirmation of importance. The car, in a way, was incidental; he himself was better, validated as significant, verified as important.

A month later terrible noises began coming from the engine. He wasn't greatly alarmed—he would go back to his good friend, who had in fact promised a continuation of their relationship. He re-entered the same showroom where he had acquired his exhilarating sense of freedom and power and pleasure, but his friend wasn't there. The woman that had been so attentive wasn't to be found. He was directed through a door to another part of the building. It was noisy and cold. There was no place to sit. No one paid any attention to him.

He finally found someone who looked as if he might be in charge of something and was told in a surly voice that there were six people ahead of him and that he would have to wait. It took a couple of hours to make arrangements to get the engine fixed. All the time he was made to feel like an intruder who had a lot of nerve to show up in a place like that, and not only an intruder, but a very stupid intruder because he didn't know what caused the engine to make those noises. He left, finally, feeling incompetent, friendless, frustrated, helpless.

Varieties of Manipulation
Nearly everyone I know can tell a variation on that story. The product and the setting vary, but the experience is the same. We are treated as distinguished guests when we can give something. What appears as friendship is not always friendship at all; it may be a skillfully acted performance designed to put us in the frame of mind in which we will buy a product that will enrich the seller. Once the transaction is completed, the performance is terminated. The experience is common in places of business, education, government, hospitals, schools, homes—and churches.

In fact, it may take place in churches more often than any other place. That, however, is no good reason for avoiding the church. I don't refuse to enter an automobile showroom, even though I am aware of the manipulative nature of the place. I don't refuse to enter a hospital, even though I know that very often the primary interests of many who work there are not mine. And I don't refuse to enter a church just because I know how easily and frequently the language and rituals of religion are put to the service of hypocrisy, self-aggrandizement, self-righteousness and controlling others. But I am on my guard.

The Galatian Christians were in the middle of just such an experience, and Paul knew that it was bound to turn out badly. They were not yet aware of the consequences, but it would not be long before they would be suffering them.

At the time that Paul wrote to them they were still basking
in the genial warm glow of Judaizing blandishment. Paul,
a battle-scarred veteran in such matters, blows the whistle
on the operation.

*My dear friends, what I would really like for you to do is try to put
yourselves in my shoes to the same extent that I, when I was with you,
put myself in yours. You were very sensitive and kind then. You did
me no wrong. You were well aware that the reason that I ended up
preaching to you was that I came down with that repulsive eye ailment and, prevented from continuing my journey, was forced to
stop with you. That is how I came to preach to you. And don't you
remember that even though many people interpreted my illness as
some kind of demonic affliction, and even though taking in a sick
guest was most troublesome for you, you chose to treat me as well as
you would treat an angel of God—as well as you would treat Jesus
himself if he had visited you. What has happened to the satisfaction
you felt at that time? There were some of you then who, if possible,
would have traded eyes with me—that is how deeply you cared! And
now have I suddenly become your enemy simply by telling you the
truth? I can't believe it. These heretical teachers go to great lengths
to flatter you, but their motives are rotten. They want to shut you out
of the free world of God's grace so that you will always depend on
them for approval and direction, making them feel important. It is a
good thing to be ardent in doing good, but not just when I am in
your presence. Can't you continue the same concern for both my
person and my message when I am away from you as you had when I
was with you? Do you know how I feel right now and will feel until
Christ's life becomes visible in your lives? Like a mother in the pain
of childbirth. Oh, I keep wishing that I was with you, then I wouldn't
out of sheer frustration be reduced to this blunt, letter-writing
language.*

*Tell me now, you who have become so enamored with the law,
have you paid close attention to the law? Abraham, remember had
two sons, one by the slave woman and one by the free woman. The
son of the slave woman was born by human connivance; the son of*

the free woman was born by God's promise. This illustrates the very thing we are dealing with now. The two births represent two ways of being in relationship with God. One is from Mount Sinai in Arabia, it corresponds with what is now going on in Jerusalem—a slave life, producing slaves as offspring—this is the way of Hagar. In contrast to that there is an invisible Jerusalem, a free Jerusalem, and she is our mother—this is the way of Sarah. Remember what Isaiah wrote,

> *Rejoice, barren woman who bears no children,*
> *Exclaim and cry out, woman who has no birth pangs,*
> *Because the children of the bereft woman*
> *Now surpass the children of the chosen woman.*

Isn't it clear, brothers, that you, like Isaac, are children of promise? Isn't it clear also that just as in the days of Hagar and Sarah, the child of faithless connivance (Ishmael) harassed the child of the faithful promise (Isaac), so the harassment that you are experiencing from the Jerusalem heretics follows that old pattern? There is a scripture to tell us what to do: "Expel the slave mother with her son, for the slave son will not inherit with the free son." Isn't that conclusive? We are not children of the slave woman, but of the free woman.

Freedom in Necessity

"They make much of you, but for no good purpose; they want to shut you out, that you may make much of them" (4:17). Which is to say, "They are flattering you, but they have no interest in leading you into a deeper freedom; they are only interested in what they can get from you. And when they get it you are not going to see them anymore or hear from them again. They only want to use you. If you permit yourself to be used, you are back in the same old life again, the life of slavery. Don't listen to them! I know that their words are appealing. I know that what they say is plausible. But their motives are base. They do not want you to get to the place where you are complete and whole, but to the place where you will spend your money and play the part that lines their pockets, feeds their egos and promotes their causes."

The religious product being promoted by Judaizing interpolators was more self-control, more self-determination. If we engage in particular rituals and keep certain rules, we always know where we stand. If we know what we can do that will make us more acceptable in God's eyes than a person who doesn't do them, we, by doing them, can advance our status. Such a religion puts us in control. We no longer have to live by faith, trusting to God to accept us in mercy. We no longer have to live in love toward our neighbor, trusting, often against all appearances, that that neighbor is God's child. What we are being offered is a security system in which we do not have to live by faith, will not have to trust in God, but can trust instead in ourselves.

Freedom is the bait commonly used in getting people to respond to such lures. If I control my relationship with God, the argument goes, I am freer than if God controls it. If I control my relationships with others, I am freer than if they control them. If I can remove all ambiguity in my relationships, know exactly where I stand, am self-determined, that gives me a sense of freedom. All the features that the Judaizers emphasized served this function. Take circumcision, for instance. One is either circumcised or not—there are no shades of gray. There is a visible scar, proof of a relationship with God. At the same time it defines relationships with others, setting one either with or in contrast to every other person. The mysteries of faith and the vulnerabilities of love are pushed into the background. Doctrinal formulations, moral codes, emotional rituals function similarly to circumcision. The people who offer them are selling a system of self-definition, implying an increase of freedom, but "for no good purpose; they want to shut you out." The end result of following that line is enslavement to another's ego ("that you make much of them"), not a developing freedom in God's will.

All that talk is fantasy. Despite the emphasis on the practical, it is surrounded with an aura of unreality—the soft seduction of trendy narcissism. The Galatians were being offered a security system in which they would not have to live by faith, would not have to trust in God, but could trust in themselves. Paul counters it by recalling the actual experience that they, Paul and the Galatians, had shared together. When he first came to them he was physically ill. He was hurt and in trouble. They knew that he was on his way to some other place and only stopped in Galatia because he was forced to by his illness. That couldn't have been very flattering to them. Paul was spending time with them only because he wasn't able to be where he had wanted to go. Not only that, but his illness was a considerable inconvenience to them. He did not come as a strong, charismatic, glamorous leader with impressive credentials, offering sweeping, glorious solutions. He was weak and in need of their help. Paul didn't come among them and dazzle them with a sales pitch. He arrived and immediately fell apart; they had to nurse him back to health.

Paul is not explicit about the nature of his illness.[1] If he is speaking literally in the sentence "if possible, you would have plucked out your eyes and given them to me" (4:15), his trouble may have been an eye disease accompanied by a repulsive discharge. But regardless of the kind of illness, Paul's point is that while he was preaching the gospel to them, they were engaged in acts of sacrificial service to him, offering themselves in practical expressions of love.

He did not come to them as one in control of his life; he was dependent on their hospitality. And they let themselves be tied down in helping him. From both sides, the situation would not seem to increase a sense of freedom. Paul was forced by his illness to change his plans and preach in Galatia. The Galatians were forced to spend long hours in caring for a sick man. And what, in fact, did they experience in the process? Deep satisfaction (verse 15). They were freely doing good; Paul was preaching the freedom of Christ.

Packed into the single word *satisfaction* is a vivid reminder: freedom does not come by getting control of things or people but by freely assenting to the reality of being, whether that being is a stranger's illness, or a crushing disappointment, or an incomprehensible failure, or a futile desolation. We discover the meaning of the free life in acts of compassion and loving service, not in running after people who make big promises to us. We realize the life of freedom in Christ by accepting pain and trouble and ailments, not in grabbing after the smooth solutions to life proposed by celebrities or experts. The moment of Paul's disabling illness and the Galatian's compassionate care was one of the glorious times in their lives: they knew freedom those days. They were hemmed in by necessities—Paul couldn't go where he had intended; the Galatians were pressed to tend to Paul's needs—and there resulted profound satisfaction. Freedom comes from trusting, not from manipulating, from leaving matters to God rather than trying to be in control.

Tangled in Our Own Plans
Paul reinforces what they had learned together in that experience by recalling the well-known story of Isaac and Ishmael. It is also a story about the freedom that comes when we trust God to be in control and the loss of freedom that results when we attempt to take control ourselves.

The famous promise to Abraham was that he would be the father of the faithful and that all the nations of the earth would be blessed in his offspring. But there was a problem: Abraham did not have a child. All he had was a promise that he would have a child. The years piled up. Still no child. God promised but there was nothing to show for it. Besides, there was a biological absurdity at the heart of the whole business: Sarah was an old woman, and barren.

If ever there was a situation in which it seemed like a clear case for God helping those who help themselves, this was it. Abraham and Sarah unable to conceive a child, conceived a plan: Sarah's young maid, Hagar, would bear the child. The plan was full of common sense. It was agreed and acted upon. Hagar became pregnant and Ishmael was born.

A few years later Sarah conceived and gave birth to Isaac.

The interrelated births of Isaac and Ishmael are treated carefully and meditatively in Genesis. Out of the multiple meanings in the stories of the two sons, Paul selects a single truth and uses it to drive home his message on freedom: one son was born because God promised, the other son was born because Abraham and Sarah doubted. Ishmael was a product of human impatience, the human trying to do God's work for him; Isaac was the result of God doing his own work in his own time. Ishmael caused nothing but trouble; Isaac continued in the faithful covenant of the freely loving God. The great disaster of Abraham's life was that he used Hagar to get what he thought God wanted for him; the great achievement of his life was what God did for him apart from any programs or plans that he put into action.

The lesson of that old piece of history is clear enough: the moment we begin manipulating lives in order to get control of circumstances, we become enslaved in our own plans, tangled up in our own red tape, and have to live with grievous, unintended consequences—Ishmael's descendants complicated the life of faith enormously for centuries. The life of freedom is a life of receiving, of believing, of accepting, of hoping. Because God freely keeps his promises, we are free to trust.

Bound Until We Trust

Any word, any occasion, that promises to help us to live out more than we are now experiencing, to escape the humdrum, to banish the boredom that seeps into our days, to defy the monotony that plagues our routines, to assert ourselves as free creatures who do not slavishly march in lockstep with the crowd—any such word catches our attention. It catches our attention and rouses our desire because we are created to live freely. Freedom is a basic condition of our wholeness. We are not made to live in cramped conditions. We are not so constructed that we can be satisfied with feelings of impotence and insignificance. We are made "little less than God."

If buying a new car will help us escape, we will buy the car. If anointing ourselves with a new cologne or perfume will banish boredom, we will anoint. If reading a new book will help us assert ourselves, we will read away. If embarking on a new program will put us in control of our relationship with God, we will sign up. Gerald May is blunt: "Even religion, the one timeless gate to beyond-the-self, becomes a technique. A means to an end for self-improvement. To create better behavior, to make more abiding happiness, to manufacture holiness. There are times when through religion one comes close to turning over self-control. Offering it up. Giving up. Sacrificing the delusion. But even then, most often, it becomes the turning over of a defective self to the ultimate fixer in the sky, in the hopes of getting a rebuilt and perfected self in return. This is not going beyond self, nor is it giving up. It's using God to help one get back in control."[2]

No one has understood this better than Paul. He knew that we are not whole persons until we are free, and that we are not free until we trust. He faced the reality that religion repeatedly falls prey to the insatiable will of human beings to do and control, and thus makes a mockery of that freedom. And he proclaimed, with rare power and effectiveness, that God in Christ has set us free from that compulsion so that we can be free in that original created sense: free to live in a praising, trusting relationship with God, free to live in a loving, serving relationship with other persons. He also understood that there are people all around us who will appeal to our need and appetite for freedom to get something from us that they want for themselves—control.

Few people are willing, or able, to accept us just as we are and then to encourage us in being who God created us to be and who we can be by his mercy. There are open and secret attempts to use us, to manipulate us, to enslave us to someone else's program or agenda or cause. And so at the same time that Paul encourages us in a life of uninhibited faith, of reckless trust in God, he warns against believing the lies of persons who promise much but give little, who, as soon as they get us into their camp and get our names signed on the contract, disappear and shut us out of their lives.

For freedom Christ has set us free; stand fast therefore, and do not submit again to a yoke of slavery.

Now I, Paul, say to you that if you receive circumcision, Christ will be of no advantage to you. I testify again to every man who receives circumcision that he is bound to keep the whole law. You are severed from Christ, you who would be justified by the law; you have fallen away from grace. For through the Spirit, by faith, we wait for the hope of righteousness. For in Christ Jesus neither circumcision nor uncircumcision is of any avail, but faith working through love. You were running well; who hindered you from obeying the truth? This persuasion is not from him who calls you. A little leaven leavens the whole lump. I have confidence in the Lord that you will take no other view than mine; and he who is troubling you will bear his judgment, whoever he is. But if I, brethren, still preach circumcision, why am I still persecuted? In that case the stumbling block of the cross has been removed. I wish those who unsettle you would mutilate themselves!

Galatians 5:1-12

---

11   Free to Stand

IN CHRIST WE ARE FREE to take a stand. A space has been cleared in the thick forest and brambles of necessity from which we can freely respond to God, freely grow in the image of God, freely develop in relationships of forgiveness. Having been provided the space, we are free to take a stand there. Taking a stand fights drifting with the tide. Taking a stand contrasts with being carried and coddled by the culture. Taking a stand means standing on our own two feet.

The gift and experience of freedom is a piece of ground from which we can assert initiative. It must not be relinquished. It was won in a hard fight. Christ gave his life in victorious battle for this piece of real estate. It must be preserved. Nothing and no one may be permitted to encroach upon it. Every Christian must preserve the stance of freedom on this ground. *Ich kann nicht anders.*

Paul is absolutely certain that we are set free: freedom is fact. He is also genuinely alarmed that freedom may be lost. The history of God's dealings with his people is marked by losses of freedom, often through sheer negligence. Paul, addressing persons who have been set free for a life that can only be developed in an atmosphere of continuing freedom, does well to warn and exhort. Without determination and vigilance and attention, freedom will certainly be lost.

It is for a free life that Christ has set us free. So take your stand! Never again let anyone put a harness of slavery on you.

I am emphatic about this. The moment any one of you submits to circumcision, at that same moment Christ's hard-won gift of freedom is squandered. I repeat my witness: the person who accepts circumcision trades all the advantages of the free life in Christ for the obligations of the slave life of the law.

I suspect you don't intend this, but this is what happens. When you attempt to live by your own religious plans and projects, you are cut off from Christ, you fall out of grace. Meanwhile we expectantly wait for a satisfying relationship with God through the Spirit. For in Christ Jesus, neither our most conscientious religion, nor our disregard of religion, amounts to anything. What matters is something far more interior: faith working through love.

You were running superbly! Who cut in on you, deflecting you from the true course of obedience? This detour doesn't come from the one who called you into the race in the first place. And please don't toss this off as insignificant; it only takes a minute amount of yeast, you know, to leaven an entire loaf. Deep down, in the Lord, I am confident that you will not defect. But the one who is upsetting you, whoever he is, will bear the divine judgment.

As for the rumor that I continue to preach circumcision (like I did in those pre-Damascus Road days), that is absurd. Why would I still be persecuted then? If I were preaching that old message, the scandal of the cross, its very integrity and identity, would be nullified. Why don't these agitators, obsessive as they are about circumcision, go all the way and castrate themselves!

Air of Freedom

Freedom is a new experience. It is not what we are used to. It is not what we grew up with. It is not what we are accustomed to seeing around us. There is unexpected freshness. Jesus identified his ministry "to proclaim release to the captives . . . to set at liberty those who are oppressed" (Lk 4:18). Every Christian, thus emancipated, lives in this liberty.

But the air of freedom is as unfamiliar as it is exhilarating. Unpracticed as we are in the life of freedom, we are unaware and unalert to the many ways it may be lost. We are like the person who has spent a long time behind prison walls. His life has been completely controlled and regulated by the terms of his punishment. His clothes, his food, his sleep, his work, his recreation have all been dictated by prison officials. Then he is set free. He stands outside the prison walls with a new suit of clothes, a little money—and his freedom. The freedom is exhilarating. Long dreamed of, it is now experienced. But the man cannot stand there forever and savor his freedom. He must do something with it. What will he do? He now has the task of living in a free society. But the free life is something to which he is neither accustomed nor trained. It has been a long time since he has experienced freedom. How will he use it? The first days and weeks of the free life are perilous. Many do not survive them. Recidivism is extremely high among discharged prisoners. They do not know what to do with their freedom. They have been conditioned by another way of life. After a few attempts and failures, they often relapse into old ways and return to the security of the prison.

In Christ we are declared free. In Christ we experience freedom. What do we do with it? We are free from the past with its guilts and inhibitions and punishments. We are discharged with a clean slate from the dungeon of self and prejudice, fear and sin. But we cannot stand forever just taking in the free air and whistling tunes of freedom.

Slaves of the Past

Deeply embedded in Paul's imagination is a classic story of God's gift of freedom and the ease with which the freedom is lost. For Paul, a "Hebrew of the Hebrews," the exodus story is pivotal in any understanding of freedom. Even though he does not make explicit reference to the story here, it is so potent in the devout memory that it cannot fail to have been prominent in Paul's alarm over the ease in which freedom can regress.

The story begins with God's people in a quagmire of slavery in Egypt. They have been there for four hundred years. These are people whose ancestor Abraham began the great venture of living by faith, leaving what he knew and possessed in Ur for what he believed and expected in God. These are people whose ancestors had roamed the desert, their life histories saturated with God. It was a struggling existence, full of agonizing doubts and painful disciplines. It was also an invigorating existence, packed with meaning and taut with purpose. There was suffering and there was blessing, but most of all there was vitality—Abraham, Isaac, Jacob, Joseph were alive at every level. Out of their deepest beings extraordinary expressions of humanity blossomed in acts of worship and faith.

Then, seemingly, it all disappeared in a swamp of slavery. The immense Egyptian system of bureaucratic religion and politics swallowed them up. They were assimilated into the anthill society of Egypt, carrying bricks, quarrying stone for arrogantly pompous tombs and building cities and palaces that to this day stand as monuments to the bloated vulgarity of their oppressors. Instead of living a free life under the Palestinian stars, listening to the voice of God, worshiping and praising, they toiled under the whips of slavemasters, were demeaned by the curses of cruel rulers and were dehumanized in the impersonal machinery of slavery.

The contrast is enormous and cannot be overdrawn. For the patriarchs God was the initiating, activating, providing, creating word. They lived in a universe that was dominated by God. God called. God promised. God blessed. They lived, in other words, by faith. Their descendants in Egypt lived in a world that was dominated by work. Men, not God, told them where to live, what to do, how to worship. When God had dominated their lives they lived free; when man dominated their lives they lived enslaved.

This world of slavery was also a world of religion. Egypt was the most religious culture the world had ever seen. All the architecture was religious. All the organization was religious. The motivation for all the building projects was religious. The art was religious. The politics were religious. The Egyptians had an extraordinary intelligence and a well-organized priesthood. Their wisdom was subtle and mature; their learning was immense; their accomplishments remain to this day awesome. Theirs was a religion designed to make things happen: it guaranteed a happy immortality; it controlled (supposedly) the rising and falling of the Nile so that the land would be fertile; it controlled the people's every move so that there would be law and order. The Egyptians talked about God, addressed prayers to God, built temples for God; but religion in Egypt was always what *they* were doing. Egypt was a thoroughly religious society, and Egypt was a thoroughgoing slave society.[1]

Then the Hebrews were delivered from Egypt. Moses was raised up by God to be their leader. There were lengthy and complex negotiations with the Egyptian Pharaoh, the handsome, steel-willed Rameses II. Promises were made and then retracted. Then, against all odds, when the repeatedly dashed hopes of the people seemed beyond revival, they were delivered. One day they were a demoralized and unarmed people crushed under the cruelty and

whim of an enslaving religion; the next day they were vic-
toriously free, singing the praises of a redeeming God.
They left their slave life behind them. They also left, it
turned out, a comfortable security, a sophisticated culture,
a spectacular beauty and a dependable routine. In the
desert wastes they were absolutely dependent on a God
whom they could not see. There were no pillared temples
for worship and no granaries from which they could get
their allotment of food. All they had was their freedom, a
few prayers and songs to an invisible God, and a precarious
diet of manna and quail.

Moses led them across the hot sands to Sinai, a gigantic
volcanic mountain in the Arabian desert, where they
camped and began a life of learning what it meant to be
God's people. Here they would be trained in living as free
people and not as slaves, discover what it means to live by
faith and not by works, realize what it means to live under
the provident blessing of God and not under the tyranny
of a pharaoh. For four centuries they had been building
grandiose tombs to hold a few mummified corpses; now
they would go to work building a living community of faith.

Charter of Freedom

Moses climbed the mountain to receive God's revelation.
He returned with the Ten Commandments, the constitu-
tion and bill of rights for a people who were then to live the
free life of faith. Some people mistakenly look at those commandments as restrictive, not realizing that for those who
first heard them (and for those who even now hear them in
faith) they provided for and preserved the values of the
free life. The reality and truth of God is protected from
commercialization and manipulation. Human life is honored. The dignity of work is protected. Close, personal
relationships are preserved. Truth is respected. Each of the
commandments articulates and protects a reality without

which the free life is not possible.

For the life of freedom and faith is not caprice and whim; it is not randomness and chance. The lives of these people were no longer to be subject to the moods and will of the strongest person. Their work was no longer to be fodder for the megalomaniac ambitions of a pharaoh. Each person is of eternal value in himself, in herself.

The charter of freedom was proclaimed. Now these people would begin the lifelong task of living free by faith. After an interlude of worship and celebration (Ex 24), Moses went back up the mountain to receive instructions for the day-by-day routines that would support and develop a life responsive to God's love and salvation, instructions regarding the routines of worship and relationship and community. He was gone a long time. The people became restless and bored. Nothing was happening. They weren't going anyplace. There was nothing to do. There was nothing to see.

They knew that they had been set free. They had all shared that experience; it was incontestable. They were going to learn to live by faith, live in relation to the vast but invisible reality of God, learn to center their lives in voluntary worship not in compulsory slave labor. But day succeeded day and there was nothing but emptiness. Moses was gone. They didn't realize that the emptiness was prerequisite to the new learning. Impatiently, the people began to make demands. They came before Aaron and said, "Up, make us gods, who shall go before us; as for this Moses, the man who brought us up out of the land of Egypt, we do not know what has become of him." We are tired of waiting. We will wait no longer. We are tired of nothing; we want something. Make us gods.

They did not want to live by faith but by sight. "Israel will no longer trust the God who is appearing to Moses on Sinai, but desires a visible God to lead them on their way."[2]

They did not want to live in response to God but wanted
gods that they could use to get what they wanted, like they
had had in Egypt—gods one could move around and use
to make things happen. In Egypt, of course, it hadn't
worked to their benefit, but that was only because they
didn't own the gods; the Egyptians owned them. But now
that they were free of Egypt they wanted some gods that
they could possess, gods they could use to augment their
freedom, display their pride, fulfill their ambitions.

So Aaron made them a golden calf—Apis, the highly
esteemed bull god of Egypt.[3]

Moses came down the mountain carrying God's word on
stone tablets, saw the appalling trivialization of the free
life ("the people sat down to eat and drink, and rose up to
play"—Ex 32:6), in hot anger threw the tablets to the
ground and broke them, and pulverized the golden calf.

People are always looking for a religion that has no demands, only rewards, a religion that bedazzles and enter-
tains, in which there is no waiting and no emptiness. And
they can usually find someone around who will help them
construct some sort of golden-calf religion. God provides
a large, beautiful and complex creation as an environment
in which we can live to the glory of God. God provides a
painfully achieved, deeply wrought redemption so that we
can experience the love of God. "For freedom Christ has
set us free!" Then, in a moment of boredom, we turn our
backs on all of that and say to someone or other, "Make
us gods." Entertain us; pamper us; amuse us. Give us some
supernatural gewgaw that we can play with. We abandon
the awesome silence of worship and fill the air with tire-
some discussions of circumcision or uncircumcision. We
get tired of the strenuous life of freedom and faith and
regress to the old slave religion that reduces God to a decoration or an amulet or a scar. We buy some religious idea
or practice that we think will eliminate the pain of being

human, banish all moments of emptiness and waiting. A living faith is traded in on an infantile religion. In stupidity or sloth we degrade and diminish our lives by abandoning the clear ground of freedom and dabbling in practices which entangle us in the brier patches of old emotional dependencies and spiritual superstitions.

Paul is angry the way Moses was angry—and for the same reason: "You were running well; who hindered you from obeying the truth?"

The Threat of Religion
The gravest threats to the free life do not come from the atheist or the secularist. They come from the quarter we might least suspect—from religion, particularly a former religion, a childhood religion, a neurotic religion. Living in the free air of freedom with its insecurities and chilling breezes, we are subject to sudden nostalgia for the warm, secure, swaddling clothes of an earlier religion—little borrowings from the past, inconspicuous compromises with the environment: an Egyptian calf-god, a Judaistic circumcision, sentimentalized prayers, stereotyped emotions, formula explanations. Religious friends suggest or insist on ways to improve or correct or legitimize our life before God. We satisfy our need for security or admiration or relief from boredom. But these seemingly well-meaning additions or apparently inconsequential lapses gradually erode the base of freedom, reducing the space which Christ has made large in liberty. (Noel Coward once sent a picture post card of the Venus de Milo to a little girl and wrote across the bottom: "This is what will happen to you, if you don't stop biting your fingernails.")

Will we stand fast or will we submit to a yoke of slavery? There is no question but that a well-padded yoke of slavery can seem very attractive when we are faced with the austere risks and challenges of the free life. "Once the Christian has

set foot on the road leading out of the land of slavery,"
warns Berdyaev, "he must not sacrifice the primacy of spirit
and his original freedom and become the plaything of
necessity and compulsion."[4] Judas Iscariot was a man set
free by Christ who failed to stand fast in that freedom. He
was liberated from a past of small and selfish ambition. In
his years of association with Jesus he experienced the wide-
ness of an eternal vision, the thrill of an unconquerable
hope, the strength of an indomitable faith. He was called
by Jesus and marked as a pillar for the new community that
would bring good news and deliverance to a lost and suffering world. He was among that company of persons freed
from the prison of their sins, whose guilt was remitted and
who were learning the glorious liberty of the children of
God. He experienced no coercion in his time with Jesus.
Along with the other eleven, he was the freest person in
the world. And then, somehow, he submitted again to a
yoke of slavery. The details of the submission are not clear.
From all accounts it seems not to have been a defiant rebellion but an inattentive atavism. Was it simple greed for
money? Was it a latent lust for political intrigue, activated
by the stress and stimulus of passover week crowds? Was it
spiritual impatience attempting to provoke Jesus into mes-
sianic action? Whatever the reason, this is clear: Judas used
the freedom which Christ gave him to destroy his liberator.
The consequence was slavery. Yoked under a colossal burden of grief and guilt, he made his last mocking gesture of
freedom by committing suicide.

The Summons of the Thunder
Paul's memory holds a gallery of tragic pictures of persons
who, having been set free, inattentively failed to practice
their freedom and returned to slavery. The ancient memory of his people at Sinai, the early Christian loss of Judas,
recurrent instances in his own ministry: "certain persons

have made shipwreck of their faith, among them Hymen-aeus and Alexander" (1 Tim 1:19-20), "Demas, in love with this present world, has deserted me" (2 Tim 4:10).

The imperative is urgent: "Stand fast." His anger is hot against those who threaten freedom. Because an imposed circumcision had come to symbolize for Paul this loss of freedom and defection from the life of faith, he aims his polemic against those who insist on it. Hans Dieter Betz remarks on the timidity of the translations that avoid Paul's earthy language: "The correct interpretation is found in Luther's commentary of 1519, following Jerome. JB: 'Tell those who are disturbing you I would like to see the knife slip.' "[5]

The Galatians were familiar with the religious cult of Cybele-Attis and its castrated priests, toward whom there was public disgust. He caricatures the rite of circumcision by salting his ridicule with a reference to castration: "As for these agitators, they had better go the whole way and make eunuchs of themselves!" (NEB). Later Paul would write to the Philippians, "Beware of those who insist on mutilation—'circumcision' I will not call it" (Phil 3:2 NEB).

Freedom is no peripheral concern for Paul; it is central. It cannot be taken for granted; it must be vigorously guarded. It is not something that can be put in a bank vault and kept safe. It is not a privilege conferred, like an academic degree, that certifies access to privileges and honors. Each day we must take up the stance of freedom again. If we fail to stand deliberately and consciously, the freedom will be lost. As Ellul writes, "New acts of freedom are incessantly required. There is no such thing as a state or an acquisition in this matter. Reality encircles me. The sacred hems me in. I have to respond afresh to the summons of the thunder."[6]

For you were called to freedom, brethren; only do not use your freedom as an opportunity for the flesh, but through love be servants of one another. For the whole law is fulfilled in one word, "You shall love your neighbor as yourself." But if you bite and devour one another take heed that you are not consumed by one another.

But I say, walk by the Spirit, and do not gratify the desires of the flesh. For the desires of the flesh are against the Spirit, and the desires of the Spirit are against the flesh; for these are opposed to each other, to prevent you from doing what you would. But if you are led by the Spirit you are not under the law. Now the works of the flesh are plain: fornication, impurity, licentiousness, idolatry, sorcery, enmity, strife, jealousy, anger, selfishness, dissension, party spirit, envy, drunkenness, carousing, and the like. I warn you, as I warned you before, that those who do such things shall not inherit the kingdom of God.

Galatians 5:13-21

12   Free to Love

THE WILDERNESS, IN THE American imagination at least, is the place of freedom. There are no fences telling us where we cannot go, no traffic lights ordering us to stop and go, no roads defining the route we will take, no billboards insisting on what we must buy. As such, the wilderness attracts us—it is the place where we are given ample range to be free. It is both place and atmosphere, geography and symbol. As rules and regulations crowd in upon us, squeezing and standardizing us, the presence of the wilderness preserves a margin of primitive innocence beyond the asphalt. It preserves the unexpected and pristine, the virgin and the mysterious. The wilderness is breathtaking; it is also awesome. We are not safe in the wilderness. The wilderness has many ways to kill us. There are millions of acres of land set aside as wilderness areas, but there are also millions of people who won't go near them, and understandably so, for in the wilderness are wild animals.

One of the wildest of animals is the grizzly bear. Bears as a family are wonderful animals. They have qualities and characteristics that endear them to us. They are lazy, cuddlesome, big and soft, ambling and unhurried, comic and playful. They can be domesticated for circus acts and fictionalized for children's stories. Winnie the Pooh and the Three Bears are everyone's favorites.

The grizzly has these qualities, but with something else added—the grizzly is incurably wild. These bears are incredibly beautiful, but completely unpredictable. They are impervious to domestication. Often genial, but just as often violent, they are remote and awesome beasts— wild and free.

In the country in which I grew up, the grizzly has a vice grip on the imagination. Every native has a repertoire of grizzly stories to tell the visitor. We love telling the stories, but we hope that we are never in the stories. We want the grizzly, but we don't want him. He is marvelous, but he is also dangerous. I was walking on an alpine trail in the Rocky Mountains a few years ago with my daughter, and suddenly we saw a grizzly in a meadow below us, tearing up the turf and eating the tubers of glacier lilies. It was her first sighting of a grizzly, this immense animal of clumsy grace and elegance. We were both glad to see him, but afraid to linger. We wanted to continue to watch but feared that he would see us and lose interest in his vegetarian meal. So after a few minutes Karen said, "Let's get going." We got going. A mile or so down the trail she said, "I got two prayers answered today. I saw a grizzly; he didn't see me."

Essential but Dangerous
Paul approaches freedom with this same ambivalence: the free person is essential but dangerous. Albert Camus, in his Nobel Prize acceptance speech, is of the same mind,

"Liberty is dangerous, as hard to get along with as it is exciting."[1] So at the same time that Paul insists on freedom he cautions the free person: "For you were called to freedom, brethren; only do not use your freedom as an opportunity for the flesh." Paul engages us with the details of that tension.

It is absolutely clear, isn't it, that it is to the free life that you have been called? So make sure that you don't use this freedom as an excuse to do what you want to do and dissipate it; rather use it to serve one another in love and so strengthen it. For everything we know about developing freedom is summed up in a single sentence: Love your neighbor as yourself. If you bite and ravage each other, watch out—in no time at all you will be annihilating each other.

My counsel is this: live freely, animated and motivated by God's Spirit. Refuse to feed the compulsions of selfishness. For there is a root selfishness in us that is at odds with a free spirit, just as the free spirit is incompatible with selfishness. These two ways of life are antithetical, so that you cannot live at times one way and at times another way according to how you feel on any given day. Why don't you choose to be led by the Spirit and so escape the erratic compulsions of a law-dominated existence?

It is obvious what kind of life develops out of trying to get your own way all the time: repetitive and loveless sex, a stinking accumulation of mental and emotional garbage, frenzied and joyless grabs for happiness, trinket gods, magic-show religion, paranoid loneliness, cutthroat competition, all-consuming-yet-never-satisfied wants, a brutal temper, an impotence to love or be loved, noisy bickering, small-minded and lop-sided lifestyles, a vicious habit of depersonalizing everyone into a rival, uncontrolled and uncontrollable addictions, ugly parodies of community. I could go on.

This isn't the first time I have warned you, you know. If you use your freedom this way you will find yourself quite outside God's kingdom.

Trying to Cage Freedom

There are recurrent demands that the grizzly problem be
solved by locking the bears up, putting them in cages in
zoos. We would still be able to look at them and admire
them, but no one would get hurt. Yes, but they wouldn't
be free. You cannot exhibit freedom by putting it in a cage.

And there are recurrent demands that the problem of
personal freedom be solved by social coercion—moral
cages in a totalitarian zoo. Some people dream of making
a political and social system so perfect that no one will have
to be good. Yes, but we would no longer be persons.

We cannot domesticate freedom. There are unpredictable energies in it that are of its very essence. If we are
going to have the deep excitements of freedom, we also
will have to live with the risks of freedom. Paul is not naive
about freedom; he is not innocent in regards to freedom.
He knows its dangers, but he is also adamant as to its importance: "You were called to freedom, brethren, only do
not use your freedom as an opportunity for the flesh, but
through love be servants of one another."

Freedom is given to us and it will not be withdrawn: "You
were called to freedom." Now, what will we do with it?
Will we use it as a license to defy restraints, release inhibitions, mutilate others, loot and plunder, wallow in self-
indulgence? We must not. "Do not use your freedom as
an opportunity for the flesh."

The matter of freedom is never in question. No one ever
has too much freedom. Freedom must not be rationed.
Freedom must not be retracted. Freedom continues at the
center of Paul's exposition of the nature of life in Christ.
But freedom is not a thing in itself complete. It is an opportunity. The word *opportunity (aphormē)* in earlier strata of
the Greek language was used to designate a point from
which to launch a military attack.[2] Given this launching
place, how will you use your freedom? That is the question

to which Paul provides focus and clarification. Each detail of freedom is an aspect of opportunity. Freedom is not a state in which we are inert; it is an atmosphere in which we make active choices. Freedom is to the Christian what a brisk breeze is to a sailor—it makes the day worthwhile and exciting, but it also requires vigilant and alert decisions at sail and rudder.

Responsibly Free

There were people in the early church who argued that since Christ has set us free and that salvation is by grace, nothing we do can possibly contribute anything to God's work. That leaves us free to do spontaneously whatever we feel like doing. In every generation since, the position has never failed to find someone to give it strident exposition. A hundred years ago the feminist Victoria Woodhull used the slogan "Untrammeled Lives!" to parade doctrines of irresponsible self-indulgence.[3] W. H. Auden gave a wonderful parody of the position in his lines, "I like to sin/God likes to forgive/the world is admirably arranged."[4]

So even the most casual reading of human history shows that there is nothing excessive in Paul's caution, "do not use your freedom as an opportunity for the flesh." Throughout human history there are stories of revolutionary activity that begin gloriously with people set free only to end ingloriously in ignominy. After the freedom is won, the free people, exhilarated by the wine of freedom but immature in the ways of freedom, indulge in profligate rioting and violent lust. Others, alarmed by the explosion of wild freedom in these lives, herd them into cages of custom and morality and put a dictator on guard at the door.

The gospel way of dealing with the dangers of freedom is quite different: "Through love be servants of one another." "How does this freedom come to realisation in us?" asks Schlier. "The decisive answer is in love. It is not in isolation but in life with others that the Christian attains to freedom."[5] The best way, the only way, finally, of expressing the life of freedom is in an act of love. Only love expresses freedom in ways that enhance rather than destroy, in ways that enliven rather than deaden.

The word *love,* as it is used in the biblical texts, has two obvious qualities. St. John, the master teacher on love (just as Paul is the master teacher on freedom), taught that love has its origins in God ("we love, because he first loved us" —1 Jn 4:19) and that it is a relationship with persons ("beloved, if God so loves us, we also ought to love one another" —1 Jn 4:11). Love is not a word that describes my feelings; it is not a technique by which I fulfill my needs; it is not an ideal, abstract and pure, on which I meditate or discourse. It is acting in correspondence with or in response to God in relation to persons.

Each person is God's person, standing before God as his child and before me as a brother or sister. "All men," wrote William Law, "are great instances of divine love, therefore let all men be instances of your love."[6] This person does not stand before me as an obstruction or a threat or an affront. If I cannot see the person in relation to God, then I am not free to love. I will either want to get rid of her because she is in my way, or I will want to use her in order to get my own way. Either way I lose freedom.

John warns, "Do not love the world or the things in the world" (1 Jn 2:15). It is a parody of love to depersonalize it by loving in general, that is, loving the world; and it is a parody of love to love material objects, that is, the things in the world. Love is aware of and responsible to *personal* connections, divine and human, freely chosen.

Apart from love, freedom quickly disintegrates into the anarchy described in the book of Judges when "every man did what was right in his own eyes" (Judg 21:25). In that book the most horrible story in all of literature is told

—the story of Jephthah's daughter—documenting with chilling realism Paul's warning "if you bite and devour one another take heed that you are not consumed by one another."

Paul gives fifteen one-word illustrations of persons who "bite and devour one another" behind a screen of freedom. *Fornication* detaches the freedom of sexuality from the reality of intimacy and destroys it. *Impurity* divides the immediacy of the common from the holy and profanes it. *Licentiousness* separates festivity from community and banalizes it. *Idolatry* disconnects worship from the mystery of the Trinity and commercializes it. *Sorcery* severs means from ends and trivializes everything. *Enmity* isolates outrage from its context in righteousness and balloons it into war. *Strife* rends genial desire from the values of goodness and makes ruthless competition of it. *Jealousy* empties freely offered admiration of its inner core of reverence and leaves it a green-eyed monster. *Anger* splits a natural yearning for justice from the great body of truth and leaves it merely bad-tempered. *Selfishness* cuts the legitimacy of personal need adrift from the continental necessities of social concern and abandons it to insularity. *Dissensions* splinter pieces of the finite from the infinite and make chaos. *Party spirit* partitions off one favorite truth from the mansion of truth and narrows it into bigotry. *Envy* disengages the elements of diversity from their design in the hierarchy of being and reduces the lot to bargain-basement utility. *Drunkenness* divorces appetite from nourishment and forges chains of addiction. *Carousings* sunder ecstasy from liturgy and result in nothing but headaches and nausea. Reality with its origins in God and consequences in persons is ignored. Things that God joined together are put asunder and become violations of freedom. "Take heed that you are not consumed by one another." There is no connectedness, therefore there is no freedom, though for a moment there is a grinning, hopping parody of it.

Paul's list is random and formless, like the actions themselves. Paul rips the masks off propagandizing phrases like "self-expression," "freedom to be yourself," "doing your own thing," and uncovers the deceptions that promise liberation but do not fulfill it. Sin never admits to its true character. "The devil is a liar and a conjurer too." Each of these acts pretends to freedom but violates the reality of freedom that has its source in the love of God and flows outward toward the love of another. In place of deeply organic connectedness there is arrogant defiance of God and ruthless disregard for persons. Reality is ravaged and freedom is destroyed. Throwing tantrums is not freedom. Plundering is not freedom. Freedom acts within the cosmos of reality; apart from that cosmos, inner and outer, freedom is abused and diminished, violated and corrupted, whether from stupidity or wickedness.

The one act in which we can engage that avoids, on the one hand, straitjacketing freedom, and, on the other hand, goading freedom into anarchy—the danger of prim domestication, the danger of savage bestiality—is the act of love. It is the only other way. Freedom that is not expressed in love annihilates: "We must love one another, or die."[7]

Love is the free act that a person, once having practiced it, knows is the one act worthy of a creature made in the image of God. Freedom expressed in love is neither safely tame nor wastefully prodigal. Love and only love holds the deep, wild beauty and uncalculated energy of the natural creature in tension with the sane coherence and vibrating poise of robust, developed spirituality.

Freedom achieves humanity and avoids bestiality only when it is used in acts of love. "Freedom without love," says Ellul, "resembles a blind man without a guide."[8] Love is the only act able to incorporate the wildness of the spontaneous with the beauties of faithfulness. It is an act of fulfillment not of detraction. Each of the deflections from freedom listed by Paul destroys essential aspects of reality in the assertion of the self. Love is the free act that fulfills.

The Free Act Supreme

Paul quotes Leviticus for authority: "You shall not hate your brother in your heart, but you shall reason with your neighbor, lest you bear sin because of him. You shall not take vengeance or bear any grudge against the sons of your own people, but you shall love your neighbor as yourself: I am the LORD" (Lev 19:17-18). Hate and vengeance, in contrast to reason and love, are reactions, not free actions. They are determined by what the neighbor does, not by what I decide. Reason and love are free acts; hate and vengeance are conditioned responses.

"The whole law is fulfilled," says Paul, "through love." Grammatically, the word *fulfilled* is in the perfect tense. As such it means the whole law has been fulfilled every time one person loves another as himself. Love ... as yourself. To love my neighbors as less than myself is to treat them as a means to my ends. To love them as more would set them up for using me as a means to their ends. One way is as much a violation of love as the other, and as destructive of freedom. The command protects my freedom as much as yours, yours as much as mine. No one sacrifices freedom at the expense of the other. All become increasingly free.

For love is the free act supreme. It directs our best intentions and our best abilities to the other. It marshals our best energies into companionship and friendship with a person whom God has singled out for love. The act is not controlled by feelings or circumstances, by prejudices or customs. We are free to love the person who is presented as an enemy, the person who is designated as insignificant, the person who apparently has nothing of interest or worth to me, the person who insists on making himself unpleasant

to me. It is a great freedom to love. It means the freedom
to be myself, uniquely, totally and affirmatively with this
other.

The Spirit of Love

As we explore the reality in which we are free to love we
find that there is both an active and a passive quality to our
actions. Paul elaborates: "But I say, walk by the Spirit."
Love is a deliberate act: we walk. It is not floating on a fluffy
cloud; it is not the sudden acquisition of wings; it is not
early retirement to an armchair in paradise. We walk. We
use feet-on-the-ground things like intelligence and wisdom, Scripture and tradition. If we do not engage in this
deliberate, directed action, we are subject to pressures,
inner and outer, that re-enslave us. Without plan, without
direction, without purpose we simply trade slaveries. It
happens often. G. K. Chesterton pilloried the women's
liberation movement in England by saying, "Ten thousand
women said, I won't be dictated to—and went out and became stenographers."

The active walk is balanced by the passive "led by the
Spirit." We are not in control of all that goes on. The person, no matter how strong and gifted, is never "captain of
my fate . . . master of my soul." There is a raging storm
between the flesh and the Spirit that is played out internally
and externally. Even so, we are not rag dolls thrown back
and forth between hurricane forces. Stronger than the
force of the storm is the Spirit who leads us "beside still
waters." The freedom to love is maintained as we submit
to the Spirit who leads. We experience some dimensions
of freedom only when we are not *doing* but simply *being*—
being directed, being addressed, being loved, being led.

The free act that expresses itself in love is not a matter
of vigorously gathering all our energies of free will and
releasing them in an explosion of passionate good will. Nor

is it relaxing in the lotus-field ambiance of cosmic love and being moved to love. It is born out of relationship with God in Christ—not out of our own nature, not out of the nature of the world—a relationship in which both our activities and passivities are reborn.

Paul explains: "Walk by the Spirit, and do not gratify the desires of the flesh. For the desires of the flesh are against the Spirit, and the desires of the Spirit are against the flesh; for these are opposed to each other, to prevent you from doing what you would." Which is to say, we can't follow impulses, either God's good impulses (Spirit) or our bad ones (flesh). We would like to do what we feel like doing when we feel like doing it. We would like to not think, not decide, not plan, not agonize. We suppose that would be freedom. We are, though, only fantasizing. We are imagining not freedom but its opposite. We are imagining something like the freedom of a tree that responds to every breeze, bends before every wind, drops its leaves on signal from the autumn sun, forms buds on command from the rising sap in spring. Is the tree conscious of these marvelous expressions of life? Is any of this *decided*? We enjoy the tree but the tree does not enjoy us. There is life, glorious life, in the tree, and persons share many of the ingredients of that life, but the human being is something far more than that. One of the aspects of the "far more" is freedom.

Sometimes I want to be free the way my dog is free. I fantasize a dog's life because my dog is not subject to anxieties. But my dog is not free—she is a creature of instinct and reflex. It is not possible for her not to do most of what she does. The instincts are powerful within her, the conditioned reflexes thoroughly imposed upon her. And my leash is frequently there to restrain and guide her. It is a simple, happy life with many pleasures and delights. But it is not free.

The human is what the tree is and what the dog is, but

also more. Far more. We are free to love, free to respond to a relation with God and to develop a relation with persons that share goodness in acts of love in the rich connectedness of things. These free acts enhance, develop, complete, create.

Quiet Love

The freedom that comes from a life of faith has a quietness and naturalness to it. It is not assertive or ostentatious. It is like muscular agility in a craftsman or athlete—economically used, hardly noticeable, shaped to a purpose, not like a boy flexing his biceps before a mirror.

I don't think that we discover this primarily in the passionate acts of love that immerse us in a sea of ecstasy. For the most part we must not look for it in the dramatic, in the parade or in the honeymoon. We must express it in the minute decisions we make in regard to our feelings and gestures and words when we are with a friend or a child or a spouse or an enemy or an acquaintance or a stranger. We are equally free to plan an elaborate gift or casually to express a complement, to engage in a deeply prayed intercession or to venture a spur-of-the-moment encouragement.

Such acts do not any more come from the strenuous efforts of a powerful will than they do from a drifting abandonment to impulse. They come from exploring the balanced, rhythmic dynamics of walking by the Spirit and being led by the Spirit.

We are free to do that. We really are. We are not vegetables that mindlessly sway and flutter before the winds of custom or culture. We are not slaves of deep, primitive instincts over which we have no say. We are not conditioned by our society so thoroughly that there is no margin for unexpected and new infusions of love.

Such freedom is not freedom absolute. There is a large

trunk and root system of physical, emotional and mental givens. There are powerful instinctual drives within us that it cannot be ignored or shut off. There are powerful conditioning elements in our upbringing and social environment from which we will never be free. But, said Goethe, "By his restrictions the master proclaims himself."[9] At the last minute, as it were, when everything else has done its work and made its contribution, there is the freedom to change a tone of voice, to write a sentence in a letter, to make a telephone call—the freedom to love that will "fulfill the law."

But the fruit of the Spirit is love, joy, peace, patience, kindness, goodness, faithfulness, gentleness, self-control; against such there is no law. And those who belong to Christ Jesus have crucified the flesh with its passions and desires.

If we live by the Spirit, let us also walk by the Spirit. Let us have no self-conceit, no provoking of one another, no envy of one another.

Brethren, if a man is overtaken in any trespass, you who are spiritual should restore him in a spirit of gentleness. Look to yourself, lest you too be tempted. Bear one another's burdens, and so fulfil the law of Christ. For if any one thinks he is something, when he is nothing, he deceives himself. But let each one test his own work, and then his reason to boast will be in himself alone and not in his neighbor. For each man will have to bear his own load.

Galatians 5:22–6:5

13   Free to Create

IN THE FIRST ART CLASS I have any memory of, I was handed a piece of paper on which there was the outline of a dog, an Alaskan husky. I was instructed, along with the rest of the class, to use a black crayon to trace the outline so that it was very clear. Then I was told to fill in the outline with a color of my choice, but warned to stay inside the lines. The warning was forcibly and repeatedly expressed.

Week after week we followed the same procedure. I don't know whether my teacher drew these sketches herself or reproduced what was drawn by another. What I do know is that my part in the process was to trace the outline, and then stay within it. Art, for me, was a careful exercise in staying inside the lines. Creativity was limited to choosing from the twenty-four colors in my Crayola box, and exerting various degrees of pressure on the paper. If my crayon slipped, or through carelessness I wandered outside the lines, my work was unacceptable.

I got quite good at that, at least as I remember it, but lost interest in the process and grew to loathe art class.

Later in life I discovered that not all art classes were conducted that way. I have seen teachers tie smocks on children, put several colors of paint before them, stick a piece of newsprint on an easel and a paintbrush in their fingers, and let them loose to draw and paint whatever they wished. Wild combinations of colors and forms would come into being on the paper. Unpredictable, and sometimes quite beautiful, pictures were painted. I heard these teachers praise and admire the work of the young artists.

I have listened to some of these teachers contend, with many illustrations and arguments, that every child is a natural artist. Creativity, they say, is innate in all of us and only needs opportunity and encouragement to be expressed. But most of us have it bred out of us. If we were given the right materials and provided with the proper environment and stimulus, all of us would be artists, realizing and enjoying the energies and results of creativity.

I believe that. I believe that we were not put here to copy someone else's drawing. I believe that our highest function is not to fill in the colors of someone else's outline. I believe that we are made in the image of God and that because God is a creator, we are creators.

Our early experience often does not encourage that. We are instructed to stay within the lines. In school and church, at home and at work, we are handed someone else's outline and told to learn, pray, play, work—whatever— within it. The intimidation is appallingly successful.

In Christ we are set free to create. He sets us free to live —toward God, with people, in the world—as artists, not as copiers. He sets us free to use the stuff that God gives us to live something original.

There are always people around who insist that the task of life is to make the outlines clear and then tediously color in someone else's drawing. Sometimes these people get into the church and speak so solemnly that we think that is surely what God wants. But it isn't what God wants. "A struggle must be waged for the originality, the first hand character, of moral acts."[1] God wants us to live creatively. One of the things that Christ has done is to set us free to create.

What happens when we live God's way? Quite without any effort on our part things begin to appear in our lives much the same way that fruit appears in an orchard, things like affection for others, exuberance about life, serenity. We develop a willingness to stick with things, a sense of going with the grain of the universe, a conviction that a basic holiness permeates things and people; and we find ourselves involved in loyal commitments, not needing to force our way in life, able to marshal and direct our energies wisely. No one can make us do these things; at the same time no one can prevent us from being such persons. These qualities of life develop as surely as fruit on a well-cultivated tree. Among those who belong to Christ Jesus, everything connected with getting our own way and mindlessly responding to what everyone else calls necessities, is killed off for good.

Since this is the kind of life that we have chosen, let us make sure that we do not just hold it as an idea in our heads or as a sentiment in our hearts, but work out its implications in every detail of our lives. That means we will not compare ourselves with each other as if one of us were better and another worse. We have far more interesting things to do with our lives. Each of us is an original.

Live creatively, friends. If someone falls into sin, forgivingly restore him, saving your critical comments for yourself. Stoop to the level of those who are oppressed and share their burdens, so completing Christ's law, for if you think you are too good for that, you are badly deceived. Make a careful exploration of who you are and the work you have been given, and then sink yourselves into that. Don't live vicariously. Each of us must take responsibility for doing the creative best we can with our own lives.

Unwritten Scripts

I regularly meet people who have the idea that living by faith means being an actor in a play for which the script is already written. They try for a part and, if accepted, are assigned a role, learn lines and attend rehearsals until their parts are perfected. These people sense no freedom to make their own movements or to speak their own lines, but they seem assured that if their strings are firmly attached and their lines are nimbly spoken, their performance will be heartily applauded.

But life in Christ is nothing like that; it is free and redolent with creativity. "The world," says Berdyaev, "was made not only created, but creative."[2] Something quite remarkable takes place when we live by faith. When we believe that God has created us in his image, when we trust that he loves us and works out his salvation in us, when we decide that the only way in which life takes on meaning is when we believe that the invisible truth is what keeps the visible world together, certain things begin to happen in our lives apart from our working at them. They surprise us with their presence. God who created us continues to work creatively in us. He keeps bringing new qualities, new realities, into our lives.

Creative work requires materials. A painter needs canvas and a palette of paints. A sculptor needs clay and marble and chisels. A potter needs a wheel and clay. A conductor needs instruments and musicians to play them. What do persons need to create new forms of life in and around them? Love, joy, peace, patience, kindness, goodness, faithfulness, gentleness, self-control. We do not, like God, create *ex nihilo*, out of nothing. We need materials to work with. And we have them.

When Paul listed the consequences of living by compulsion (5:19-21), the list was random and anarchic. Fifteen items were named. The list was as disorderly in arrangement as in content. The law of sin produces lawless disorder. Paradoxically, a life determined by compulsions results in chaos, while a life of freedom falls naturally and easily into designs of beauty. For when Paul lists the results of living freely in response to God, the list is balanced and symmetrical—three groups of three items each, the number three being the most symmetrical of numbers. A three-legged stool cannot wobble.

The first three items name free acts of God that are experienced in the life of human freedom: *love,* the truth that I am accepted just as I am; *joy,* the discovery that exuberance and vitality flow freely from God's life into my life; *peace,* the realization that God works through the disparities and contradictions of my experience and brings them into harmony. Each of these comes from God. Each comes prior to either my deserts or my capacities. God is "long beforehand with my soul."

The second group of three names freedoms associated with personal growth: *patience,* the freedom to stay with something or someone, not hurrying, not rushing for a result; *kindness,* the freedom to deal with life in a relaxed and leisurely fashion, not forcing, not coercing, not pushing and shoving; *goodness,* the freedom to see and respond to life in terms of its good creation rather than in terms of its willful rebellion, confident of a basic Genesis 1—2 reality under all Genesis 3 disruptions.

The third group of three names aspects of our freedom as it is actively articulated in the world: *faithfulness,* the freedom to be involved in long-term, loyal commitments based on invisible values and meanings rather than immediate and tangible self-interests; *gentleness,* the freedom to abjure promethean assaults on the recalcitrant world

and to be instead salt and light and leaven; *self-control,* the
freedom to discipline and direct our energies wisely, impervious to whim and impulse, barometric pressures and stock-
market quotations, delivered from what Philo described
as "helpless and poverty-stricken undiscipline."[3]

The first item, love, completes the Hebrew Torah. The
last item, self-control, fulfills the Greek ideal. The Spirit
provides everything—every grace, every means—for acts
of free creation.

Spiritual Fruits

These nine materials are described under the metaphor
of fruit. Fruit is the result of a long organic and living process. The process is complex and intricate. Fruits are not
something made, manufactured or engineered. They are
not the product of the drawing board. They are not the
invention of a genius. They are not the product of a sophisticated technology. They are the results of a life of
faith created by God.

The person who lives a life of faith finds fruits appearing
in unlikely places at unanticipated times. That is, we find
that there is far more to our lives than we bring to them.
Fruit is the appropriate metaphor. We do not produce it
by our own effort. We do not purchase it from another.
It is not a reward for doing good deeds, like a merit badge,
a gold medal, a blue ribbon. Fruits are simply there. Sometimes we experience them in another, sometimes in ourselves. We live in a world that is mostly result, and so we
live in adoration, in awe, in reverence.

These nine items are also like fruit in that they are perish-
able. They spoil. They are beautiful to observe but cannot
be kept on display for long. They must be used—eaten and
digested. Fruit is something our bodies use to supply the
nutrients to live well. Just so, the Spirit gifts are what we
take into our lives so that we are able to live creatively.

A World-Garden of Creativity

Clearly, we are created and we walk in a world-garden of creativity. Creation is the environment in which we live. Still the plaint is heard, "But I'm not a creative person. Create what? I wouldn't know where to start." Just because I am created, just because I live by the fruits of creativity, doesn't mean that I am free to create." But the biblical evidence counters, "Yes, it does."

One of the profound definitions of the meaning of being human is that we are made "in the image of God" (Gen 1:27). When we look carefully at the verses in Genesis that precede that definition, we learn that the God in whose image we are made is a God who creates. "The characteristic common to God and man is apparently that: the desire and the ability to make things."[4] Berdyaev sees this freedom to create at the exact center of what it means to be human: "God created man in his own image and likeness, i.e., made him a creator too, calling him to free spontaneous activity and not to formal obedience to his power. Free creativeness is the creature's answer to the great call of its creator. Man's creative work is the fulfillment of the Creator's secret will."[5] Every person, in other words, is a creative person.

Our Kingdom Go

Paul makes the transition from the fruit-producing work of God in us to the creative work we ourselves do by announcing that "those who belong to Christ Jesus have crucified the flesh with its passions and desires." The uncreative life is a life of passions and desires, a life of impulse and necessity, a life responding to signals from others, a life of captivity to internal compulsions. It is a life that proceeds along well-charted, predictable lines—copying what others do, imitating stereotyped behavior, expressing itself in a few sentimentalities mass-produced from the cliché factories of popular culture.

Before genuine creative work takes place there must be a withdrawal from what other people demand, from routines and habits, from what voices, within and without, tell us to do. The flesh must be crucified. Wise spiritual guides in these matters refer to this action as mortification. It is a process well known to artists—those who create with words and paints, stone and sound—and to saints—those who create with the nine spirit fruits.[6]

We begin by *not* doing. We separate ourselves from what is expected, what is needed, what is possible. Creation is not copying, not filling an order, not meeting a need. It is risking oneself in the new. In order to do the creative new we must divest ourselves of the uncreative old—old habits, old reactions, old expectations, old accomplishments. Aldous Huxley, commenting on the common, uncompromising agreement of creative people on the necessity of this flesh crucifixion, writes, " 'Our kingdom go' is the necessary and unavoidable corollary of 'Thy kingdom come.' For the more there is of self, the less there is of God. The divine eternal fulness of life can be gained only by those who have deliberately lost the partial, separative life of craving and self-interest, of egocentric thinking, feeling, wishing and acting."[7]

It is difficult to do. It is easy to slip back into the familiar and undemanding world of copybook maxims. Paul warns against veering away from the free creative life that is before us and returning to deadening, imprisoning routines: "Let us have no self-conceit, no provoking of one another, no envy of one another." Creativity does not come from vaunting oneself; it does not come from setting oneself competitively against another; it does not come from wanting to be like another in any way.

Creative work begins in not doing, in "self-naughting." There must be an emptying of all uncreative, and creation-destroying ways. We are presented with a variety of materials ("fruits") with which we are free to create, but before we are free in ourselves to be creators we must "have crucified the flesh with its passions and desires." Compulsions and distractions must be set aside before free, creative work begins.[8]

In Visions Begin Responsibilities

Create what? Paul gives three examples. "Brethren, if a man is overtaken in any trespass, you who are spiritual should restore him in a spirit of gentleness." We are free to live creatively by forgiving. Forgiveness is an immensely creative act. Condemning is simply reactionary, responding in kind to an offense. Condoning is simply lazy, avoiding the difficulties of dealing with what is wrong in the world or in persons. Gentle forgiveness is the work of an artist, using the Spirit gifts in skilled and disciplined interaction with the hurt and harassed, the maimed and the rebellious. When we forgive we do creative work. We do not try to stuff a person into a precut mold. We do not disdain to work with unpromising material. We quiet ourselves into a consciousness of the creative materials with which we have to work, into an awareness that we, made in the image of God, are creators; and then we proceed to do the creative work of forgiveness that we have been called to by our Lord.

"Bear one another's burdens, and so fulfill the law of Christ. For if any one thinks he is something, when he is nothing, he deceives himself." We are free to live creatively by helping. When we need to keep ourselves rigidly upright in order to prove to ourselves and the world that we are upstanding, we are not free. But when our identity and salvation come from the life of Christ, we are free to stoop to the level of the person who is crushed under too heavy a burden, to lift that person up and to accompany him or her onward. We are free to bend, to put ourselves in the company of those who are fallen. Our Lord was free to do such creative work, eating with tax-collectors and prostitutes, receiving women as close companions in his work, touching lepers and wasting time with children. He was unrestricted by the straitjacketing of public opinion. Creative people are not connoisseurs who walk through the art galleries of the world and collect the best pictures; they are the ones who involve themselves in the stuff of the world and *make* the best pictures. This process of steeping ourselves in the elemental experiences of life, getting under the burdens of personal existence in order to share the creative, resurrection energies of the Spirit is profoundly and typically Christian. It is what Irenaeus understood God to be doing in Jesus: "He became what we are so that we might become what he is."[9]

"But let each one test his own work, and then his reason to boast will be in himself alone and not in his neighbor. For each man will have to bear his own load." We are free to live creatively by being responsible. Tolstoy was annoyed by people who thought they were creative, talked incessantly about it, but never did anything creative. He said, "If you ask a man if he can play the violin, and he says, 'Well, I suppose so, but I've never tried,' you laugh at him. But everyone talks of doing things beyond what they are now doing—with people, for people—but they never develop the personal responsibilities with which creativity is expressed."[10]

There is a double truth in Yeats's line "In dreams begins responsibility."[11] One truth is that the dream is the creative ground of the responsible life. The corresponding truth is that the responsible life, if it is to be anything more than mediocre plodding, requires dreams to give it zest and scope. Dreams are creative. The energies and motives that fuel a career of responsible living flow from dreams.

But it is mature responsibility that develops, not dreaminess. There is an appalling waste of creativity when we do not "bear our own load," but run around and pick up the loads of others. A person in a John Fowles novel comments on one of these people, "I think she's trying to solve the world's problems as a substitute for facing one or two of her own."[12]

"Bear one another's burdens" in verse 2 and "each shall bear his own burden" in verse 5 appear to be in contradiction. But a different Greek word lies behind the English *burden* in the two sentences. There is not a great deal of difference in meaning between the two words, but enough to suggest that there are times when an accumulation of burdens (*barē* in the plural) crush us to the ground and we need help, and at the same time that the inevitable pressures of life are a burden (*phortion* in the singular) and we had better learn to bear them. It is yet another aspect of creativity to discern between the two.

These three examples are provocative jabs toward creativity. They are not ditto outlines that each must color with the crayons of personal ethical behavior. They are prods, stimulating the creative awareness that original works of grace are possible in the everyday work of forgiving the sinner, in helping the hurt and in taking up personal responsibilities. Gianbattista Vico's aphorism is Pauline: "one understands only what one can create."[13] Creation continues. The streets and fields, the homes and markets of the world are an art gallery displaying not culture, but new creations in Christ.

Let him who is taught the word share all good things with him who teaches.

Do not be deceived; God is not mocked, for whatever a man sows, that he will also reap. For he who sows to his own flesh will from the flesh reap corruption; but he who sows to the Spirit will from the Spirit reap eternal life. And let us not grow weary in welldoing, for in due season we shall reap, if we do not lose heart. So then, as we have opportunity, let us do good to all men, and especially to those who are of the household of faith.

Galatians 6:6-10

14   Free to Give

I WANT TO DO IT MYSELF. It started at an early age. I
don't remember the details but I can reconstruct the picture. I began life helpless, unable to care for myself, unable
to move myself, unable to feed myself, unable to protect
myself. Gradually I acquired abilities to do things for myself: clutch a spoon, stagger from one chair to another, bite
the hand that fed me. My mind developed. I figured things
out. It was nice to have someone around to help me in the
essential acts of living, but it was even nicer to get to the
point where I didn't need any help. Years of shifting relationships followed. I became stronger, more capable,
more self-sufficient. The adults around me trusted me
more, respected me, released me to my own ways. Then
the final break. I was on my own—autonomous. My own
salary. My own car. My own apartment. No one to tell me
to brush my teeth. No one to impose an outside judgment

on whether I was dressed warmly enough. Independent.

Independent. Isn't that everyone's goal? We don't want reminders of the years when we were helpless. We don't want doubts thrown on our capacity to do things for ourselves. If someone helps us that is a sign that we are weak, that we are inadequate, that we are immature. And there is a corollary: having arrived at the place where we think we can do without anyone's help, we think everybody ought to do without our help.

If we are successful in becoming independent, we enjoy it for a while, but only for a while. We find that there are unforeseen consequences to the independent life. If we are a person without needs, we soon become a person without companions. If I become free from my parents, free from my children, free from my friends, free from God, I am not free at all but merely lonely. Isolated.

The gospel creates another kind of freedom for people who like to be independent: in Christ we are set free to give.

Be very sure now, you who have been trained to a self-sufficient maturity, that you generously enter into a common life with those who have trained you, sharing all the good things that you experience.

Don't be misled: no one makes a fool of God. What a person sows, that is exactly what he reaps. The person who sows selfishly, ignoring the needs of others—ignoring God!—reaps a crop of corruption. But the one who sows in response to God, letting God's spirit do the growth work in him, that person reaps a crop of real life.

So let's not allow ourselves to be fatigued in doing good. At the right time we will reap if we don't give up and quit. Right now, therefore, every time we get the chance, let us work for the benefit of all, starting with the people closest to us in our community of faith.

Needs and Gifts

"Let him who is taught the word share all good things with

him who teaches." Freedom is not self-sufficiency but a shared life. The ideal is not independence but interdependence. The goal is not efficient operating units but freely open and loving, freely giving and receiving human beings. The act of giving develops this free life. Martin Buber wrote: "You shall help. Each man you meet needs help, each needs *your* help. That is the thousandfold happening of each moment, that the need of help and the capacity to help make way for one another. . . . It is the nature of man to leave equally unnoticed the innermost need and the innermost gift of his own soul, although at times too, a deep hour reminds him of them. You shall awaken in the other the need of help, in yourself the capacity to help. Even when you yourself are in need—and you are—you can help others and, in so doing, help yourself."[1]

Each of us begins in ignorance and in weakness. We are taken in hand; we are led. Things are explained to us, inadequacies are dealt with, limitations realized, desires disciplined. We are weak and need strengthening. We are ignorant and need enlightenment. We are careless and need disciplining.

Each of us has strengths to share with another and knowledge with which to guide another. But that does not make us self-sufficient. If those we teach ignore us, supposing we are beyond needing anything they have to offer, we are cut off from living relationships essential to our freedom.

Sometimes we are the friend who steps in to help; sometimes we are the friend who is helped. In either case our experience of freedom is deepened. We are no longer imprisoned in our strengths; we are no longer paralyzed by our needs. We acquire a sense of mutuality as we help and are helped. We plunge into a reciprocity of giving and receiving.

There is no history of the soul that is a single unbroken

line of ascent to perfection. Peter, the apostolic rock, confessed Christ, but he also denied him. David, the man with a heart after God, sang great praises to his God, but he also grievously disobeyed him. And no history of the soul is a determined descent to damnation. Gomer was not repudiated for her faithless immorality; she was wooed and loved. The prodigal was not excommunicated from the family for squandering his life; he was welcomed and enjoyed.

Life in Christ sets us free for grace. We exist in a world of giving. God gives; we give. The unfree person must defend himself against the weakness of others by rejection, by condemnation or by denunciation, as if another's weakness were contagious and contact meant infection. Likewise the unfree person must defend himself against the strength of others by rejection, as if another's strength were domination, crushing the petals of dignity and individuality so precious to the soul.

Compassionate, generous, spontaneous mutuality develops when we realize two things: there is no even distribution of burdens in this life; there is no even distribution of strengths. The curses and the blessings are unevenly distributed. Some have heavier loads put on them than others—burdens of illness, work, family, emotional trauma. Some of these burdens we take on ourselves; some are dumped on us; some we get through sin or stupidity; some come our way through accident or mishap. But however we get them, they are not fairly or evenly distributed. And not all of us get equal strengths. Some of us are born with strong bodies and fragile emotions, others with robust emotions and weak bodies. Some acquire great strength in their homes, and others have it leeched away by their families. Some have exceptional intelligence and others barely adequate minds. There is no equality in the distribution of strengths.

Once we understand this, we will not arrogantly separate ourselves from others when we find ourselves strong, nor will we withdraw in groveling self-pity when we find ourselves weak. We will give ourselves in mutuality. The Christian is free to share both weakness and strength, burdens and abilities. Our Lord, the most complete and whole person, was not self-sufficient: Mary washed his feet; Simon of Cyrene carried his cross. Even as Jesus was carrying our burdens, some of us were carrying his.

The strong minister to the weak, but the weak also minister to the strong. The teacher is assumed to be self-sufficient or adequately compensated by a fee or an honor. But the teacher is also in need. As we acquire good things in our lives we do not become more and more independent. We do not build larger storehouses in order to preserve our riches; we find new outlets for sharing, for helping, for giving.

Manacles to the Spirit

Even in our inadequacy, even in our weakness, even in our helplessness we are free to give. But we are not free not to give. Not giving is imprisoning. Not giving reduces the scope of living. Not giving—the narcissistic obsession with the self—forges manacles on the spirit.

Paul uses a metaphor from the farm to show that a life that is spent in devotion to the self is self-destructive: "Whatever a man sows, that he will also reap. For he who sows to his own flesh will from the flesh reap corruption."

"Soon or late men sit down to a banquet of results and consequences."[2] Every word of encouragement, every prayer of intercession, every act of helping is seed which will mature to eternal life. Every word of criticism, every avoidance of compassion, every indulgence of greed is a seed that will mature to evil corruption. There is no possibility of deception in life. The uses and misuses of freedom,

private ventures done in secret through either modesty
or shame, have public results.

"He who sows to his own flesh" is the person absorbed
in himself, in herself. This way of life is encouraged by
greedy advertisers, self-indulgent celebrities and self-help
psychologists. Obsession with self necessarily pushes others
to the sidelines and assigns them the rule of validating my
self-esteem. "How do I look? How am I doing?" It is not,
though, by using people but by serving them that we increase our freedom. An admiring audience is a necessary
adjunct to the person who "sows to his own flesh" since
there is so little to be gleaned from such meager acreage.
A person all wrapped up in himself makes a very small
package.

Selfishness often disguises itself with the designation
"self-sufficiency." It is laudable, is it not, to feel good about
oneself and take care of oneself? And if I am forever med-
dling in someone else's life, I am probably in danger of
encouraging dependency and sloth, robbing them of the
delights of taking charge of their own lives. Henry Fairlie
sees through the deception. He rightly discerns that for
most people taking care of the self first is a "denial of one's
need for community with others, which is in fact a form of
selfishness, since it is always accompanied by a refusal of
one's *obligation of community* with others. The steps from a
reasonable self-concern to an utter selfishness are short
and swift. Most of the prescriptions for 'self-actualization'
today are rationalizations for an aggressive self-centered-
ness and, in some of their forms, for violent aggression
by one's self against other selves that get in the way. If it
is not aggression it is manipulation and the end is always
the same; always striking or maneuvering to take first
place."[3]

A life of self-love, self-pleasing, self-improvement and
self-serving can only end in corruption. It is unhealthy. It

is diseased. It is vanity—a preoccupation with the self in isolation from others, severed from all the organic relationships of helping and being helped, giving and receiving. It can only produce rottenness. The Greeks told the story of Narcissus to tell the same truth. Narcissus was vain and the gods punished him by making him fall in love with his own reflection, and so gazing at it he wasted away, for the reflection was nothing—had no substance to it, no nurturing in it, no *mutuality*. Narcissus loved himself and ignored the nymphs around him and atrophied to nothing. W. H. Auden commented that Narcissus "does not fall in love with his reflection because it is beautiful, but because it is *his*. If it were his beauty that enthralled him, he would be set free in a few years by its fading."[4] There are people on every street, far too many of them, who are similarly in love with their own vain reflections and oblivious to their neighbors, year by year becoming more vain, more vacant —empty. They are free from everyone and therefore completely unfree.

A Harvest of Goodness

By contrast, "he who sows to the Spirit will from the Spirit inherit eternal life." Sowing to the Spirit opposes sowing to the flesh. It is a life that is lived openly and responsibly —a life of mutuality. Spirit is that aspect of the Godhead that brings the other into relationship. It is that person of God by which we experience all that God gives. Sowing to the Spirit is participating in the community that experiences what God is giving: loving, saving, healing, caring. "Christianity," wrote von Hugel, "has taught us to care. Caring is the greatest thing—caring matters most."[5]

Because there are no quickly perceived cause-effect relationships between moral acts and quality of life, some jump to the conclusion that there are no connections at all. In spite of what can be observed over the span of a historical age, we still engage in the self-deception that the universe is random, that things are not connected, thereby relieving ourselves of maintaining a sustained, determined, persistent life of giving. Acts of giving are not like pebbles dropped in a pool that make a few temporary ripples and then sink to the bottom inert. They are not pebbles, they are seeds planted in the soil of life, and they will come up one day. The harvest is inevitable. "Be not deceived, God is not mocked, for whatever a man sows, that he will also reap." Decisions are seed. Attitudes are seed. Acts are seed. Prayers are seed. Thoughts are seed. All of it will come to harvest.

The person, though, who looks for quick results in the seed planting of well-doing will be disappointed. If I want potatoes for dinner tomorrow, it will do me little good to go out and plant potatoes in my garden tonight. There are long stretches of darkness and invisibility and silence that separate planting and reaping. During the stretches of waiting there is cultivating and weeding and nurturing and planting still other seeds. "Let us not grow weary in well-doing." The task is endless. There appears to be little reward and only meager appreciation. Giving is fatiguing. Why continue? Because there is a harvest ahead. Time ripens and bursts its pod. Paul saw Christ as the result of this long process of seed planting and harvest: "When the time had fully come, God sent forth his Son." Centuries had preceded that harvest. What if Abraham had quit because he didn't see the harvest? or David? or Isaiah? or Ezra? "These all died in faith, not having received what was promised" (Heb 11:13).

Persistent, faithful, plodding belief and hope are necessary if we are to remain free to give. Despair, which descends by dungeon steps to depression, is one of the major afflictions in our society. People seek relief from it sometimes in entertainment, sometimes in violence. Christians make their way out of it step by step, sometimes with great effort, on hardly visible footholds of sharing. The besetting temptation of the life of the Spirit is simply to quit.

Afghanistanitus

The freedom to give is often vitiated by the moral disease of Afghanistanitus, the idea that the *real* opportunities for significant acts of giving are in faraway places or extreme situations. Most of us want to be generous with our lives, but we are waiting for a worthily dramatic occasion. Meanwhile our moral muscles atrophy and our capacity for living freely diminishes. Paul has a remedy: "So then, as we have opportunity, let us do good to all men, and especially to those who are of the household of faith."

When we are free in Christ we are free to respond to the opportunities readily at hand for living the gospel in acts of "doing good." We are free from scrupulously attending to our own salvation and thus free to attend to another's needs. We are free from anxiously watching out for the big chance for ourselves and thus free to respond to any chance encounters with the people we meet. We are free from the compulsion to always look good in front of others and thus free to do demeaning or embarrassing things in helping others. We live opportunity-alert.

"Especially," says Paul, "to the household of faith." Is that selfish? Shortsighted? No. Paul doesn't direct our attention to those who are close to home because they are more deserving but because they are *there,* and he knows that the biggest deterrent to the drudgery of caring for an everyday friend is the dreaming of helping an exotic stranger. Giving from a distance requires less of us—less involvement, less compassion. It is easier to write out a check for a starving child halfway around the world than to share the burden of our next-door neighbor who talks too much. The distant child makes a slight dent in my check-book; the neighbor interferes with my routines and my sleep. In John Updike's novel *The Coup,* a U.S. embassy official Don X. Gibbs, is murdered in his attempt to deliver a great load of American junk food to the drought-ridden African land of Kush. His wife later reflects: "I've forgotten a lot about Don . . . actually I didn't see that much of him. He was always trying to help people. But he only liked to help people he didn't know."[6]

Paul will not permit us to compensate for neglecting those nearest us by advertising our compassion for those on another continent. Jesus, it must be remembered, re-stricted nine-tenths of his ministry to twelve Jews because it was the only way to redeem all Americans. He couldn't be bothered, says Martin Thornton, with the foreign Canaanites because his work was to save the whole world.[7] The check for the starving child must still be written and the missionary sent, but as an *extension* of what we are doing at home, not as an *exemption* from it.

Martin Luther, a great champion of freedom, in 1520 began his "Treatise on Christian Liberty" with two proposi-tions: "A Christian man is a perfectly free lord of all, subject to none. A Christian man is a perfectly dutiful servant of all, subject to all."[8] He developed an exposition of the double truth in this most moving and contemplative of all his writings.

A year later he lived it out. On April 16, 1521, he arrived in Worms to face one of the greatest ordeals of his life. He entered the city amid a terrific popular demonstration and then went to bed almost dead with fatigue. He was sched-uled to appear before the Diet the next afternoon to assert that in his life of faith he was "perfectly free . . . subject to none." When he woke the next morning, what did he do? Did he spend a few feverish hours putting some finishing touches on his speech, as you and I would? No. He spent that morning as a "perfectly dutiful servant . . . subject to all" visiting a dying man who had expressed a desire to see him. He heard this man's confession and administered the sacrament. We are told that in the afternoon, when he went before his accusers, he entered the hall smiling.[9] There, in a single story, is one of the deep secrets of the free life. When we are released from self-centered fears, when we learn to trust God's power instead of our own, we are free to give ourselves to others.

See with what large letters I am writing to you with my own hand. It is those who want to make a good showing in the flesh that would compel you to be circumcised, and only in order that they may not be persecuted for the cross of Christ. For even those who receive circumcision do not themselves keep the law, but they desire to have you circumcised that they may glory in your flesh. But far be it from me to glory except in the cross of our Lord Jesus Christ, by which the world has been crucified to me, and I to the world. For neither circumcision counts for anything, nor uncircumcision, but a new creation. Peace and mercy be upon all who walk by this rule, upon the Israel of God.

Henceforth let no man trouble me; for I bear on my body the marks of Jesus.

The grace of our Lord Jesus Christ be with your spirit, brethren. Amen.

Galatians 6:11-18

15 Free to Die

I SEE PEOPLE LOOSE IN THE world today who live as if they are free. I observe them closely. I find that they are subject to the same laws of gravity as everyone else. They are limited by bodies that need to be fed and clothed and rested like everyone else. They work at a living like everyone else. They obey traffic laws like everyone else. They are required to pay taxes like everyone else. They fail to achieve important goals like everyone else.

Still, within this vast network of limits, causes, restrictions and coercions, they do surprising, unpredictable, astonishing things. They act freely; they speak freely. These free acts and words are not hurled against the four walls of ordinary existence in a tantrum to prove freedom. These free acts and words are not frills on a huge bulk of necessity, like a French lace collar on a hair shirt. These free acts and words are at the center of being. They are characteristic of these persons.

Ortega wrote, "Life always carries a fatal dimension and some hint of having fallen into a trap. Except that this trap does not strangle us, but leaves to life a margin of decision and always permits us, out of the imposed situation, to achieve an elegant solution and to forge for ourselves a beautiful life."[1] These persons who enjoy and exhibit freedom, who achieve "an elegant solution," are persons who live by faith in God.

Behind these lives there lie famous arguments by great philosophers written in weighty books that prove there is no freedom, only necessity. Freedom, the arguments say, is an illusion; determinism is the reality. Also behind them are hordes of people who slouch through each day with no sense of freedom. They have submitted to a yoke of slavery. They simply react to what is required: they buy what glamorous models tell them to buy; they do what stronger personalities tell them to do; they speak in whatever clichés the jargon of the day provides them.

But despite the arguments that prove that we are not free and despite the crowds of people who exhibit dull and daily evidence that we are not free, these people live freely. They lost interest in the arguments long ago. They are not impressed by the crowds. It was an English medieval philosopher who spoke of *hilaritas libertatis,* which may be freely translated as "the alive and delighting enjoyment of freedom." Henry Fairlie, who regarding the Christian faith describes himself as a reluctant unbeliever, comments, "One is left wondering if anyone but a Christian could have said that."[2]

Oddly, the symbol these people have chosen to represent the free life is the cross, in origin the instrument of a cruelly determined death. Paul's concluding summary of the free life uses the cross as an exclamation mark.

Now, in these last sentences, I want to emphasize in the bold print of my personal handwriting the immense importance of what I have written to you. These people who are attempting to force circumcision upon you have only one motive: they want an easy way to look good before others, lacking the courage to live by a faith which shares Christ's suffering and death. All their talk about the law is gas–they don't themselves keep the law! They are highly selective in the laws that they observe; they only want you to be circumcised so that they can boast of their success in recruiting you to their side. That is contemptible! For my part, I am going to boast in nothing but the cross of our Lord Jesus Christ, by which the world is crucified to me and I to the world, setting me free from the stifling atmosphere of pleasing others and fitting into the little patterns that they dictate. Can't you see the central issue in all this? It is not what you and I do–submit to circumcision, reject circumcision–it is what God is doing, and he is creating a new thing, a free life! All who walk by this standard are the true Israel of God. Peace and mercy on them!

Quite frankly, I don't want to be bothered anymore by a continuation of these fussy and trivial disputes. I have far more important things to do–the serious living of this faith. I bear in my body scars from carrying the cross of Jesus.

May what our Lord Jesus Christ gives freely, be deeply and personally yours, my friends. Amen.

Glorying in the Cross

These last sentences begin, appropriately enough, with exuberance—the verb *glory,* sometimes translated *boast.* The free life is an overflow life, a glorying, dancing, exhilarating life. The next word, though, has to be a surprise, for what Paul chooses to glory in is "the cross of our Lord Jesus Christ." Where is the glory in that? Isn't crucifixion the opposite of the free life? Isn't crucifixion death? Violent, ugly, hate-poisoned death?

Yes, it is all that. Crucifixion lies in the world of determinism, of necessity, of fate. Crucifixion is the culmination of malice and weakness and ambition, sprinkled with some halfhearted good intentions. Crucifixion is what happens when people get their own way. Crucifixion results from men and women—most of them decent people—living decent lives, grabbing for their piece of the pie and shoving to keep their place in line. Add up everything we have in the gospels, the ingratitude of the nine healed lepers and the appreciation of the one, the full stomachs of the five thousand fed on bread and fish followed by the hard-hearted unbelief of the apostles, the bickering of the disciples and the winsomeness of the children, the complaints of Martha and the devotion of Mary, the extravagance of Mary Magdalene and the covetousness of Judas Iscariot, the enthusiasm of the Palm Sunday sightseers and the fecklessness of the Good Friday spectators, the confession and denial and tears of Peter, the mockery of the soldiers, the tears of the women, the courageous loyalty of Nicodemus, the boredom of Herod. The lives crisscross. The motives mix. The end of it all is crucifixion.

Yet crucifixion is more than this. It is God submitting himself to this. Jesus Christ, God with us, enters this world of determinism and necessity, a world where nothing works out the way we want it or plan it or expect it. Crucifixion is God participating in the interplay of biology and economics and politics and psychology and religion, not standing aloof from it, and accepting the verdict: "My God, my God, why hast thou forsaken me?" But the submission is not dumb cowardice; it is a freely chosen strategy. "The only way evil ever wins victories is by making a man retort by evil, reflect it, pay it back, and thus afford it a new lease on life. Over one who persistently absorbs it and refuses to give it out, it is powerless. It is in this way that Paul sees Christ dealing with the forces of evil—going on and on, triumphantly absorbing their attack by untiring obedience, till eventually there is nothing more they can do."[3]

This is what Paul proclaims and praises. Paul does not glory in Jesus' walking on the water, showing himself Lord of creation. Paul does not glory in Jesus' calling Lazarus from the tomb, showing himself Lord over death. Paul does not glory in Jesus' teaching the beatitudes, showing himself a master truth-teller. Paul does not glory in Jesus' touching the leper, showing himself the compassionate healer. He knows all those things and appreciates them. His life of faith is enriched by them. But he *glories* in the crucifixion. His boast is that God in Jesus entered the stuff of our everyday existence where the lights and shadows mingle, where our good intentions and evil impulses vie for ascendancy, where hope struggles with despair, where men try their best and give up, where all ends in ugliness and injustice, where life is not fair, where things don't work out for the best. Paul doesn't boast of a God glorious in the heavens, untouched by the mess and confusion and ambiguity of our history. He doesn't assemble sonorous, multisyllabled lists of God's attributes and boast that no Greek or Roman or Egyptian god has half the qualities. No. "Far be it from me to glory except in the *cross* of our Lord Jesus Christ."

Singing the Free Life
Paul extends his boast: not only will he glory in the cross of Christ because there it is revealed that God has entered into this existence where no one is free, where we are all imprisoned in the law of sin and death, but he will also glory in it because the meaning of his own life is revealed there too, for this same cross is that by which "the world has been crucified to me, and I to the world."

Paul is singing the free life, celebrating the glorious liberty of the children of God. How did he come to it? The way that Christ came to it, via crucifixion. Paul didn't become free by adding up all the courageous moral choices he had made in defiance of the Greek culture in which he had grown up. He didn't get it by accumulating learning and virtue and wisdom in the Jewish heritage into which he was born. He didn't get it by retreating into the Arabian desert where he was free from the expectations and influences of others and free to be alone with God. He didn't do it by concentrating on the good times—the times when he preached powerfully, or had clear sailing in his missionary travels, or when the words came effortlessly and clear while he was dictating one of his famous letters. He experienced freedom when he was trapped in difficulties, caught in the contradictions and paradoxes of the faith, when he was shipwrecked, imprisoned, mocked. Paul didn't seek out the comfortable jobs, didn't hide from the opposition, didn't retreat from challenge. Everywhere he was up against indifference, malice and ignorance that he simply couldn't budge. He was stuck in prison. He was interrupted by shipwreck. He was chased and beaten. A free man? All the facts are against it. And yet no one has written so convincingly, so influentially and so autobiographically on living freely. He locates the source of this free life in the cross "by which the world has been crucified to me, and I to the world." Let the world do its worst, and, when it has done its worst, we are free to find out and experience what God does. Or let the world do its best, and, when that best turns out not to be enough, we are free for what God does. Let me do my worst, and, when I have done my worst, I experience what God does. Or let me do my best, and, when my best is not enough, I am free for what God does.

What God does is to resurrect. The cross of Christ is empty. The tomb is emptied. Christ dies and sets us free to die. "In the eyes of God our dying is not simply negative, it is an immensely important and salutary thing; by living we become ourselves, by dying we become God's, if, that is, we know how to die, if we so die that everything we have

become in our living is handed back to the God who gave
us life for him to refashion and use according to his pleasure."[4] God immediately acts in his new way: resurrection.

The freedom to die is the climax freedom. "Unless a
grain of wheat falls into the earth and dies, it remains alone;
but if it dies it bears much fruit" (Jn 12:24). If I no longer
have to protect and safeguard my life, I am free to live by
faith. If I no longer have to justify my life, I am free to live
by faith. If I no longer have to dread death, fearful that all
meaning terminates in my coffin, I am free to live by faith.
"Though terrifying, the taking of death into ourselves is
also liberating: It frees us from servitude to the petty cares
that threaten to engulf our daily life and thereby opens us
to the essential *projects* by which we can make our lives personally and significantly our own. Heidegger calls this the
condition of 'freedom-toward-death' or 'resoluteness.' "[5]

The Freedom of God among Us

A great deal of freedom talk is only Promethean defiance.
It is rebellion against God rather than participation in
God's grace. This is the common misconception of freedom
that Jonathan Edwards combated in his magisterial *Freedom
of the Will*.[6] But freedom that is merely self-will is hardly
what Paul had in mind. It is not until we are free to die
that we are free to participate in the ultimate expression
of God's freedom, resurrection. This resurrection, inaugu-
rated in Jesus and preached by Paul, is not an exception
to the run-of-the-mill ordinariness of our lives, but the
promised and sure conclusion. Resurrection is not a yearly
celebration of the few lucky moments we have felt things
might turn out all right, maybe, someday. Resurrection is
not a springlike gush of good feeling that we get some
years when we have been able to forget the bad times and
suppress the hurting memories. Resurrection is not what
we get when we manage to avoid failure or when we man-

age to achieve success. It is not what *we* do at all. It is not
what *other people* do. It is what *God* does when we have done
all we can and it is not enough, when we have done all we
can and it turns out to be crucifixion. It is what God does
when we exhaust our attempts at freedom. Resurrection is
the freedom of God among us and in us.

There is no freedom worthy of the name that is developed by avoiding difficult situations or unpleasant people.
Freedom that matures out of a life of faith is not selective,
does not pick and choose. It does not ignore the hard questions and recognize the easy ones. It embraces. It includes
especially death: the death of our Lord, the death of our
friends, our children, our parents, ourselves—and all the
metaphorical deaths, little and large, in which we are severed from what we thought we could not do without, from
what alone we thought could fulfill or complete us. Faith-
freedom accepts all the necessities, all the determinisms
of biology and politics and economics and physics—crucifixion!—and goes on to experience one more thing—resurrection: God freely doing what we cannot do and we ourselves freely responding.

Bloody Truths
Paul has a great gift for expressing a complex and passionate argument in a pithy epigram. The gift is brilliantly in
use here: "Neither circumcision counts for anything nor
uncircumcision, but a new creation." Circumcision and uncircumcision are representative words in Paul's vocabulary.
In the powerful argument of 5:1-15 the two words represent two ways of life, which, in stereotype, exhibit loss of
freedom: the Jewish way that imposed a religious ritual on
all who would live well before God and the Greek way that
wanted to be let loose to play and run and pursue happiness. These two ways of life continue to be presented to us:
the morally earnest person who would help us to get to God

by loading us down with rules and procedures and advice; and the fun-loving, carefree spirit who would release us to fulfill our human potential in whatever way we feel is best.

Our society is split between these two approaches. There are people who are seriously trying to live out moral ideals and responsibilities and enlisting others in their program (the circumcised). And there are people who are convinced that their first priority is to treat themselves to a good time (the uncircumcised). They both argue for freedom. Culture is a contest between the two.

Paul refused these alternatives. While in some ways they are opposites, in one significant way they are the same: they both refuse to deal with death. They are not free to die. They are desperate to hold on to life. The uncircumcised are desperate to snatch some happiness out of fleeting days; the circumcised, desperate to preserve meaning in the chaos of a corrupt society. They are desperate because they exclude God. They are not free to die because their own life is all they know and all they believe in. The one is anxiously and compulsively moral, the other frantically and obsessively happy. An uptight morality. A humorless happiness. Neither is free. Malcolm Muggeridge reflects on a remarkable passage in Pasternak's *Doctor Zhivago* in which the hero muses that in a Communist society freedom exists only in concentration camps. "The same notion is found at the very heart of the Christian religion—that the only way to live is to die. There *is* a way of deliverance, after all, but it lies in the exactly opposite direction to the one so dazzlingly signposted by the media—out of the ego, not into it, heads lifted up from the trough instead of buried in it, the arc lights pale and ineffectual in the bright light of everlasting truth."[7]

If we are going to live freely in and for and with God, neither being good nor having fun counts for anything, but only a new creation; not keeping rules or breaking rules, but a new creation; not reviving the old-time religion or swinging with the new pagans, but a new creation; not circumcision or uncircumcision, but a new creation; not what you do, but what God does; not what I do, but what God does.

Paul's arguments have been vigorous. His language, alive in the cause of freedom, has done all that language can do. He uses words, as Charles Williams put it, "the way poets do, infusing new life into them."[8] His sentences have been sword thrusts in pitched battle. No more can be expected of an argument. All that words on parchment can do has been done. He has spared no effort, no intelligence, no emotion in this fight for the freedom to live by faith and the freedom that develops out of a life of faith.

He now announces that he is done talking about the subject and that he wants us to be done with it too. There is crucifixion to be faced. There is freedom to be lived. There is God to be enjoyed. Paul will argue when argument is necessary; he will discuss as long as discussion is useful, but what he really wants to do is get on with the life of faith-freedom. Crucifixion puts all other questions, all other concerns, into a subordinate position. Once we face the fact of death and accept it, there is a sense in which all further religious discussion is parlor talk.

"All truths," said Nietzsche, "are bloody truths for me."[9] Paul said, "I bear on my body the marks of Jesus." He didn't get them in Gamaliel's synagogue in disputation with the rabbis. He had put his body on the line and had scars to show for it. The word, in Greek, is *stigmata*. *Stigmata* in first-century Greece were brands placed on slaves to mark their status. Sometimes adherents of religious cults would have marks tatooed on their bodies to signify that they belonged to a particular god or goddess. The nail marks in Jesus' hands and feet and the sword cut in his side were understood by later generations as *stigmata*, marks of the free life arrived at through crucifixion.

Impatient with any continuation of a subject that is so clearly settled, Paul will talk no more about freedom but simply live it. There is serious, intense, joyful living to be done. The human enterprise of freedom in Christ, created to be lived out grandly, dangerously and courageously, must not be trivialized into a bull session. It is time to get on with it. "Henceforth let no man trouble me"—with questions and accusations, with anxious arguments, with cautious moralisms.

Free Indeed

We passionately believe in a living God and find the half-gods, mockers of freedom, falling along the wayside. We commit ourselves to a living Christ and discover that we are introduced into the country of freedom. We receive into ourselves the gift-bringing Spirit and realize the aptitudes and abilities for living freely. Apart from faith in God we live in a world of brute determinism, bullied by those who are stronger than we, coerced by laws that are alien to our nature, constricted by hostile forces. Or, we live in an absurd, haphazard randomness. In faith we find ourselves in a conscious and developing relationship with a free God and therefore able to experience and realize freedom ourselves, achieving "an elegant solution," forging "a beautiful life."

It was because Jesus Christ was free to die that he was able to open up the entire spectrum of the free life for us. Crucifixion was followed by resurrection. "If the Son makes you free, you will be free indeed" (Jn 8:36). The resurrection is the great, awesome, incomprehensible and yet unavoidable result of crucifixion. The absolute determinism of death becomes the unlimited freedom of resurrection life. Resurrection is *there,* yet not in such a way that we can handle it, take a picture of it, weigh it, explain it.

Still, it is real. But only by faith. It is not there to be used in deterministic ways, but only to be lived in free responses. Participation in the resurrection brings about the free life of praying, praising, adoring, loving—traveling light! Resurrection is God's way of freely being with us so that we can freely be with him and with each other.

When I read the resurrection stories in the gospel records, I am always struck by the hidden, elusive, spontaneous quality in them. No one saw it happen. No camera photographed the event. The risen Lord slipped in and out of the disciples' presence. He was so unobtrusive that he was supposed at different times to be a gardener, a traveler, a beachcomber. Still, there is unanimous and emphatic agreement that it was Jesus, the Christ, who was there, alive and free. Resurrection is God among us, freely. God is not controlled by our evil or our goodness, by our doubt or our faith, our ignorance or our knowledge. God is not an object or a force that we can get possession of. God is not a truth that we can master and then use to bludgeon a stubborn agnostic friend into belief. God is not goodness that we can securely possess in a strong box. God is free. Through Christ's resurrection he is freely among us so that we live freely, free for all.

Notes

1 Free for All

[1]Ernest T. Campbell, *Where Cross the Crowded Ways* (New York: Association Press, 1973), pp. 50-51.

[2]Henry David Thoreau, *Walden* (New York: New American Library, 1960), p. 10.

[3]Will and Ariel Durant, *Lessons in History* (New York: Simon & Schuster, 1968), p. 68.

[4]Jacques Ellul, *The Presence of the Kingdom* (New York: Seabury, 1967), p. 59.

[5]Nicolas Berdyaev, *The Fate of Man in the Modern World* (Ann Arbor: Univ. of Michigan Press, 1961), p. 44.

2 Free to Live

[1]I heard the phrase in a conversation on the subject of Beckett. I do not know if it is a quotation from Beckett (I have not been able to verify it) or another's summary of him. In either case, it seems to me a completely accurate epigram of his position. There is an excellent summary of Beckett in William Barrett, *Time of Need* (New York: Harper and Row, 1972), pp. 241-77.

[2]"By these words then, 'That he might deliver us' etc., Paul sheweth what is the argument of this Epistle: to wit, that we have need of grace and of Christ, and that no creature, neither man nor angel, can deliver man out of this present evil world. For these are works belonging only to the Divine majesty." Martin Luther, *A Commentary on St. Paul's Epistle to the Galatians* (London: James Clarke & Co., 1953), p. 54.

[3]E. DeWitt Burton, *The Epistle to the Galatians* (Edinburgh: T. & T. Clark, 1921), p. 13.
[4]F. F. Bruce, *Apostle of the Heart Set Free* (Grand Rapids: Eerdmans, 1978).
[5]A. M. Hunter, *Galatians to Colossians,* Layman's Bible Commentary (London: SCM, 1959), p. 7.
[6]Erich Fromm, *Escape from Freedom* (New York: Holt, Rinehart & Winston, 1963).

3 Free to Curse
[1]T. S. Eliot defines heresy as "an attempt to simplify the truth, by reducing it to the limits of our ordinary understanding, instead of enlarging our reason to the apprehension of truth." *The Idea of a Christian Society* (New York: Harcourt Brace Jovanovich, 1940), p. 51.
[2]Hans Dieter Betz sees this curse along with the blessing at the end of the letter (6:16) bracketing the letter, "one of the special features of Paul's Galatians." *Galatians* (Philadelphia: Fortress, 1979), p. 50.
[3]Luther, *Commentary,* p. 479.
[4]George Sheehan, *Running and Being* (New York: Simon & Shuster, 1978), p. 108.

4 Free to Change
[1]*Robert Penn Warren Talking, Interviews 1950-1978,* ed. Floyd C. Watkins and John T. Hiers (New York: Random House, 1980), p. 194.
[2]Ibid., p. 181.
[3]Baron Frederich von Hugel, *Selected Letters 1896-1924,* ed. Bernard Holland (New York: E. P. Dutton, 1933), p. 174.
[4]T. H. White, *The Book of Merlyn* (Austin: Univ. of Texas Press, 1977), p. 132.
[5]Peter Berger, *The Heretical Imperative* (New York: Seabury, 1979), p. 189.
[6]Thomas Merton, *The Silent Life* (New York: Farrar, Straus & Cudahy, 1957), pp. 166-67.
[7]Randall Jarrell, "The Woman at the Washington Zoo," *The Complete Poems* (New York: Farrar, Straus & Giroux, 1969), p. 216.

5 Free to Resist
[1]"It makes a great deal of difference, as Bishop Berkeley observed, whether you put truth in the first place or the second. It makes a great deal of difference whether you say that your objective is a free society but that you wish first to be prosperous, or first to be comfortable or first to be something else, or whether you say that your objective is a free society." Archibald MacLeish, "The Conquest of America," *Atlantic Monthly,* March 1980, p. 42.

6 Free to Explore
[1]Quoted by W. E. Sangster, *The Pure in Heart* (Nashville: Abingdon,

n.d.), p. 232.

[2]T. S. Eliot, "The Four Quartets," *The Complete Poems and Plays 1909-1950* (New York: Harcourt, Brace & Co., 1958), p. 144.

[3]The summary sentence in one of the great novels of Christian ministry, George Bernanos, *Diary of a Country Priest* (Garden City, N.Y.: Image Books, 1954), p. 232.

7 Free to Think

[1]These reflections on the meaning of circumcision are my own and do not have historical parallels to corroborate them. But there is biblical precedent for using the sign of circumcision as a stimulus for theological understanding of our life in the covenant. Jeremiah preached, "Circumcise yourselves to the LORD, remove the foreskin of your hearts" (Jer 4:4). And Paul's first-century contemporary, Philo of Alexandria, developed allegorical considerations on the rite of circumcision. In its origin the rite was of limited importance, but through the centuries it "summed up in itself all the fundamental convictions of Israel's election" (W. Eichrodt, *Theology of the Old Testament,* 2 vols. (Philadelphia: Westminster, 1961), 1:139.

[2]See Burton, *Epistle to the Galatians,* p. 152, and Markus Barth, *Ephesians,* 2 vols. (Garden City, N.Y.: Doubleday, 1974), 2:448.

8 Free to Fail

[1]G. K. Chesterton, *Heretics* (London: Bodley Head, 1960), p. 13.

[2]F. O. Mattiessen, *American Renaissance* (New York: Oxford Univ. Press, 1968), p. 187.

[3]Thus: "The noun *torah* is built from the Hiphil, transitive, form of the verb *yarah. Yarah* means 'to shoot,' but the Hiphil, while also meaning such, means as well 'to teach.' When one man teaches another, he shoots ideas from his own into the other's mind. But in so doing he 'reveals' what is in his own"—George A. F. Knight, *A Christian Theology of the Old Testament* (Atlanta: John Knox Press, 1959), pp. 237-38.

[4]W. Gutbrod, νόμος, *Theological Dictionary of the New Testament,* ed. G. Kittel, 10 vols. (Grand Rapids: Eerdmans, 1964-76), 4:1045.

[5]H. Schlier, ἐλεύθερος, *TDNT,* 2:497: "Freedom from the Law thus means specifically freedom from the moralism which awakens hidden self-seeking. It means freedom from the secret claim which man makes on himself in the form of legal demand. It means freedom from the meeting of this claim in the form of legal achievement. It means freedom from self-lordship before God in the guise of serious and obedient responsibility towards Him."

[6]One of the most vulgar books to appear in my lifetime is *Success!* by Michael Korda (New York: Random House, 1977). It eliminates all relationships in life, obscures all values, subordinates everything living to the lifeless abstraction "success" and then proceeds to provide directions to perpetrate this abstraction. The most appalling thing about

the book is that no one was appalled by it. No one noticed the enormous obscenity of the book arriving week after week, without embarrassment, on the best-seller lists. People have lost all memory, apparently, of being made in the "image of God."

[7]Baron Frederich von Hugel, *Essays and Addresses on the Philosophy of Religion,* Second Series (London: J. M. Dent and Sons, 1963), p. 18.

[8]William Barclay, *The Letters to the Galatians and Ephesians,* The Daily Study Bible (Edinburgh: The Saint Andrew Press, 1962), p. 34.

[9]Lewis Thomas, *The Medusa and the Snail* (New York: The Viking Press, 1979), p. 39.

9   Free to Receive

[1]Thomas, *Medusa,* p. 115.

[2]Also see 1 Cor 6:20; 7:23; Ps 49:7-8.

[3]Joachim Jeremias, *New Testament Theology: The Proclamation of Jesus* (New York: Scribners, 1971), p. 197.

[4]George Steiner, *Martin Heidegger* (New York: The Viking Press, 1978), p. 21.

[5]Thomas Hardy, *Far from the Madding Crowd* (New York: New American Library, 1961), p. 160.

[6]Jose Ortega y Gasset, *What Is Philosophy?* (New York: W. Norton & Co., 1960), p. 244.

[7]"It seems to me that the most urgent and decisive task for Christians today, on the basis of fellowship with Christ, is to recover the full meaning of freedom." Jacques Ellul, *The Ethics of Freedom* (Grand Rapids: Eerdmans, 1976), p. 193.

10   Free to Trust

[1]Paul nowhere specifies the exact nature of his illness. His omission has been more than compensated for by his commentators. The paucity of fact has provoked a plethora of fancy. Out of all the suggestions, an eye disease seems to me most probable. Bruce Metzger has collected the extensive literature on Paul's illness in *Index to Periodical Literature on the Apostle Paul,* New Testament Tools and Studies, 1 (Leiden: Brill, 1960), nos. 242-57.

[2]Gerald May, *Simply Sane* (New York: Paulist Press, 1977), p. 13.

11   Free to Stand

[1]"How vast and beautiful were the creations of artist and craftsman in that great age of temple and palace construction! It was a time of wonderful opportunities for them. Ruined sanctuaries of past ages had to be rebuilt, and new temples in honor of the gods were constantly being ordered; the Pharaohs sought splendid new palaces which would be worthy of their great achievements. Material considerations were also favorable to the new age. *Countless prisoners of war and captured slaves placed unlimited quantities of laborers at Egyptian disposal*

[my italics] while the booty taken on the field of battle, the plunder of conquered cities, and the tribute of vanquished nations provided every possible requirement for the conduct of extensive building operations and every encouragement for the architect to undertake magnificent tasks." George Steindorff and Keith C. Seele, *When Egypt Ruled the East* (Chicago: Univ. of Chicago Press, 1957), p. 156.

[2]Martin Noth, *Exodus, a Commentary,* trans. J. S. Bowdon (Philadelphia: Westminster Press, 1962), p. 247.

[3]"Under Rameses II (the Pharaoh of the Exodus) a magnificent mortuary gallery was laid out in which the sacred bulls were buried in splendid stone sarcophagi. This subterranean cemetery—a gallery nearly three hundred and fifty feet in length carved out of the solid rock, with a row of niches for the burials of the individual bulls— the so-called Serapeum, was highly venerated as late as the Ptolemaic period, when it attracted great hosts of pious pilgrims." Steindorff and Seele, *When Egypt Ruled,* p. 141.

[4]Nicolas Berdyaev, *Dostoevsky* (New York: Meridian Books, 1957), p. 82.

[5]Betz, *Galatians,* p. 270.

[6]Ellul, *Ethics of Freedom,* p. 355.

12 Free to Love

[1]Albert Camus, "Speech of Acceptance upon the Award of the Nobel Prize for Literature," trans. Justin O'Brien, *Atlantic,* CCI, no. 5 (May 1958), pp. 33-34.

[2]*The Expositors Greek Testament,* ed. Robertson Nicoll (Grand Rapids: Eerdmans, 1970), 3:186.

[3]Dan McCall, *Beecher* (New York, E. P. Dutton, 1979), p. 59.

[4]W. H. Auden, *Collected Poems,* ed. Edward Mendelson (New York: Random House, 1976), p. 72.

[5]Schlier, p. 500.

[6]William Law, *A Serious Call to a Holy Life* (New York: Paulist Press, 1978), p. 257.

[7]Auden, *Collected Poems,* p. 154.

[8]Ellul, *Ethics of Freedom,* p. 207.

[9]Mumford, *Pentagon of Power,* p. 337.

13 Free to Create

[1]Nicolas Berdyaev, *The Destiny of Man* (New York: Harper and Row, 1960), p. 169.

[2]Nicolas Berdyaev, *The Meaning of the Creative Act* (New York: Harper and Row, 1955), p. 144.

[3]Quoted by Betz, *Galatians,* p. 290.

[4]Dorothy L. Sayers, *The Mind of the Maker* (San Francisco: Harper and Row, 1979), p. 22.

[5]Berdyaev, *The Destiny of Man,* p. 32.

[6]Aldous Huxley identified the similarity between artistic creation and the creative life of spiritual freedom: "Only the most highly disciplined artist can recapture, on a higher level, the spontaneity of the child with its first paint-box. Nothing is more difficult than to be simple. . . . It is by long obedience and hard work that the artist comes to unforced spontaneity and consummate mastery. Knowing that he can never create anything on his own account, out of the top layers, so to speak, of his personal consciousness, he submits obediently to the workings of 'inspiration'; and knowing that the medium in which he works has its own self-nature, which must not be ignored or violently overridden, he makes himself its patient servant and, in this way, achieves perfect freedom of expression. But life is also an art, and the man who would become a consummate artist in living must follow, on all the levels of his being, the same procedure as that by which the painter or the sculptor or any other craftsman comes to his own more limited perfection." *The Perennial Philosophy* (New York: Harper and Row, 1970), pp. 115-17.

[7]Ibid., p. 96.

[8]Chaung Tzu, the Chinese sage, tells a marvelous story that describes this middle movement between being given creative work to do and engaging in creative living itself: "Ch'ing, the chief carpenter, was carving wood into a stand for musical instruments. When finished, the work appeared to those who saw it as though of supernatural execution; and the Prince of Lu asked him, saying, 'What mystery is there in your art?' 'No mystery, Your Highness,' replied Ch'ing. 'And yet there is something. When I am about to make such a stand, I guard against any diminution of my vital power. I first reduce my mind to absolute quiescence. Three days in this condition, and I become oblivious of any reward to be gained. Five days, and I become oblivious of any fame to be acquired. Seven days, and I become unconscious of my four limbs and my physical frame. Then, with no thought of the Court present in my mind, my skill becomes concentrated, and all disturbing elements from without are gone. I enter some mountain forest, I search for a suitable tree. It contains the form required, which is afterwards elaborated. I see the stand in my mind's eye, and then set to work. Beyond that there is nothing. I bring my own native capacity into relation with that of the wood.' " Ibid., p. 170.

[9]Irenaeus, *Early Christian Fathers,* ed. Cyril Richardson (Philadelphia: Westminster Press, 1953), p. 351.

[10]Richard Macksey, "Scientific Creativity," *Johns Hopkins Magazine,* February 1980, p. 23.

[11]W. B. Yeats, *The Collected Poems* (New York: MacMillan, 1959), p. 98.

[12]John Fowles, *Daniel Martin* (New York: New American Library, 1977), p. 478.

[13]Lewis Mumford, *Techniques and Human Development* (New York: Harcourt Brace Jovanovich, 1967), p. 67.

14 Free to Give

[1] Martin Buber, *Pointing the Way* (New York: Harper and Bros., 1957), p. 110.

[2] Raymond T. Stamm, "The Epistle to the Galatians: Introduction and Exegesis," in *Interpreter's Bible*, ed. George A. Buttrick, 12 vols. (Nashville: Abingdon, 1953), 10:580.

[3] Henry Fairlie, *The Seven Deadly Sins Today* (Washington, D.C.: New Republic Books, 1978), p. 40.

[4] W. H. Auden, *The Dyer's Hand* (New York: Random House, 1962), p. 94.

[5] *Letters from Baron Friedrich von Hugel to a Niece*, ed. and intro. Gwendolyn Greene (London: J. M. Dent & Sons, 1958), p. xliii.

[6] John Updike, *The Coup* (New York: Alfred Knopf, 1978), p. 271.

[7] Martin Thornton, *Pastoral Theology: A Reorientation* (London: SPCK, 1964), p. 49.

[8] Martin Luther, *Three Treatises* (Philadelphia: Muhlenberg Press, 1947), p. 251.

[9] David Roberts, *The Grandeur and Misery of Man* (New York: Oxford Univ. Press, 1955), p. 46.

15 Free to Die

[1] Ortega y Gasset, *What Is Philosophy?*, p. 248.

[2] Fairlie, *Seven Deadly Sins*, p. 33.

[3] John A. T. Robinson, *The Body* (London: SCM, 1952), p. 40.

[4] Austin Farrer, *A Faith of Our Own* (Cleveland: The World Publishing Co., 1960), pp. 15-16.

[5] William Barrett, *Irrational Man* (Garden City, N.Y.: Doubleday, 1958), p. 225.

[6] Jonathan Edwards, *The Freedom of the Will* (New Haven: Yale Univ. Press, 1957).

[7] Malcolm Muggeridge, *Jesus Rediscovered* (Garden City, N.Y.: Doubleday, 1979), p. 93.

[8] Charles Williams, *The Descent of the Dove* (New York: Meridian Books, 1956), p. 8.

[9] Quoted by Rollo May, *Existence* (New York: Basic Books, 1958), p. 8.